UNIFORMS OF 1812
Napoleon's Retreat from Moscow

UNIFORMS OF 1812
NAPOLEON'S RETREAT FROM
MOSCOW

PHILIP J. HAYTHORNTHWAITE

Illustrated by
MICHAEL CHAPPELL

'*A man such as I am is*
not much concerned
over the lives of a
million men.'

Napoleon Bonaparte

BLANDFORD PRESS
POOLE   DORSET

First published in the U.K. 1976 as
Uniforms of the Retreat from Moscow 1812
by Blandford Press,
Link House, West Street,
Poole, Dorset BH15 1LL

Reprinted in this edition 1982

Copyright © 1976 and 1982 Blandford Books Ltd

ISBN 0 7137 1283 X

Set in 10/11pt Baskerville
by Woolaston Parker Limited, Leicester
Printed by
Fletcher & Son Ltd, Norwich

CONTENTS

ACKNOWLEDGEMENTS

I would like to express my sincere thanks to Mr D. Sully and Mr R. Hayhurst, for allowing me to consult material in their possession; to Mr H. V. Wilkinson of Windermere for supplying many of the rarer contemporary books; and as always to Mike Chappell for interpreting so superbly the mass of sketches and often difficult contemporary material with which I supplied him, and to Barry Gregory of Blandford Press for his constant help and valuable suggestions.

P.J.H.

AUTHOR'S NOTES

There is difficulty in establishing the 'correct' spelling of proper names, contemporary accounts and histories as well as modern works frequently giving different versions of regimental, personal and place-names. Thus can be found Semenovskaya, Semenouskoye, Semenovskoye, Semyonovka and Semenovka, all referring to a collection of wooden huts and the stream on which they stood; similarly Krasnoe, Krasny, Krasnyi and Krasnöe; Elizavetgrad, Elisabethgrad and Jelisawetgrad; Maloyaroslavets, Malo-Yaroslavets and Malo-Jaroslavitz; Kovno and Kaunas, etc.; and the battle known as Borodino to the Russians was called 'The Moskwa' (Moskowa or Moskva) by the French.

All dates are given according to the Gregorian Calendar used in Western Europe, not according to the Julian Calendar used in Russia until the Revolution; in 1812 the Julian was twelve days behind the Gregorian.

Reference should be made to the maps when consulting the brief history of the campaign which follows.

Many works are cited in the bibliography as sources for further reading, some of the most accessible being the other titles in the Blandford Press Colour Series. To make initial further reading as easy as possible, the text to certain plates contains precise references to illustrations in other volumes of the Blandford series.

HISTORICAL INTRODUCTION

Napoleon Bonaparte, Emperor of the French, became virtual dictator of western and central Europe with the conclusion of the Treaty of Tilsit in July 1807, by the elimination of two erstwhile enemies: the King of Prussia, beaten into accepting a humiliating peace, and Czar Alexander I of Russia, forced to recognize the existence of the Duchy of Warsaw and the French satellite organisation of the 'Confederation of the Rhine' (both mostly appropriated from Prussia), and to support Napoleon's 'Continental System' intended to ruin Britain's trade. Austria's capitulation after the Battle of Wagram in 1809 left only the British and nationalist armies in the Iberian peninsula resisting Napoleon.

Russia, however, resenting the revival of a Polish state, was openly infringing the Continental System. By late 1811 Napoleon had decided to force the Czar back into line and prepared an army of immense proportions in Poland, preparatory to an invasion of Russia. Its divisions were drawn from virtually every state in the sphere of French influence and (though numbers are detailed elsewhere) was roughly 675,000 strong, of whom some 450,000 men were to be used in the actual invasion. Napoleon's original plan was simple: to inflict a sharp defeat upon the Russians without advancing so far that his communications would be stretched; that and the occupation of some territory, he calculated, should force the Russians into submission.

The enormous 'Grande Armée' (named from its size) had a central striking force consisting of Italian, German and Polish contingents as well as French, and two flanking Corps under Marshal Macdonald in the north and Prince Schwarzenburg in the south provided by the 'allied' states of Prussia and Austria respectively; neither played a major part in the campaign. The central force consisted of Napoleon's own 'Main Army' (six army corps: the élite Imperial Guard, the experienced Marshal Davoût's I Corps, Oudinot's II Corps, Marshal Ney's III, and I and II Cavalry Corps under the flamboyant King of Naples, Joachim Murat); the 'Army of Italy' under Napoleon's stepson, Eugène de Beauharnais (Eugène's IV Corps, Gouvion St. Cyr's Bavarian VI Corps, and Grouchy's III Cavalry Corps); and the 'Second Support Army' commanded by Napoleon's dissolute brother Jérôme, King of Westphalia, composed of his VIII Corps, Poniatowski's Polish V Corps, Reynier's Saxon VII, and IV Cavalry Corps. Two remaining Corps, IX and XI, were held in reserve at the rear.

The Russian army, at best inefficient, was totally disorganised and could not immediately oppose the invasion. Preparations to arm the peasantry as militia or 'opolchenie' (begun in 1806) continued apace as patriotic fervour swept through society at the prospect of foreign invaders on the soil of 'mother Russia' – 223,361 peasants were enrolled in 1812 alone. Of a regular army estimated at between 518,000 and 815,000 men, comparatively few could immediately go into action, and the command situation was in chaos. The 'First West Army' (153,000 strong on paper, actually under 127,000), commanded by Minister of War Barclay de Tolly, of German-Scots ancestry and disliked by even his own staff as a 'foreigner', was stationed behind the River Niemen to cover the northern part of Napoleon's force; the 'Second West Army' of Prince Bagration, between 48,000 and 60,000 strong, was to cover the centre; and Tormasov's 'Third West Army' of about 45,000 south of the Pripet Marshes was to protect the southern flank. Other troops were not instantly available: 30,000 in Finland, 19,500 in the Crimea, 24,000 in the Caucasus, and Admiral Tschitchagov's 'Army of the Danube' (35,000) marching north. To make matters worse, the Czar's strategy was much influenced by a Prussian, Colonel von Phull, who 'lived in a world of his own imagination, and contrived to stumble over every straw that lay athwart his path'.

The result of this confusion, mismanagement and internal jealousy was that an enormous gap was left between the armies of Barclay and Bagration, which Napoleon exploited. With Macdonald's X Corps marching north to secure Riga, the invasion began on 23 June 1812 when the first elements of the 'Grande Armée' crossed the River Niemen, moving forward in three columns, a slow and tedious process occasioned by uncharacteristic caution on Napoleon's part and by the enormous amounts of baggage, supplies and camp-followers which trailed behind the army. The march was an exercise in endurance, under a burning sun and dust so thick that drums had to beat at the head of each battalion to prevent the men getting lost. As Barclay retired on Drissa, Oudinot was detached to follow, Napoleon with the main body pushing on from Vilna to Vitebsk, Jérôme and Davoût following Bagration towards Mohilev. Frantic messages from the Czar instructed Barclay and Bagration to link up, but as the latter's dislike of Barclay (his superior) was now approaching hatred the manoeuvre had little appeal.

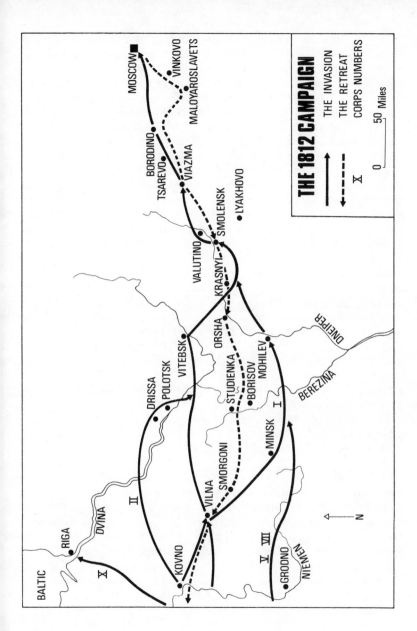

THE 1812 CAMPAIGN

THE INVASION
THE RETREAT
CORPS NUMBERS   X

0   50 Miles

BALTIC

RIGA

DVINA

DRISSA
POLOTSK
VITEBSK

II

KOVNO

VILNA

SMORGONI

MINSK

STUDIENKA
BORISOV
MOHILEV

BEREZINA

DNEIPER

ORSHA

KRASNYI

VALUTINO
SMOLENSK
LYAKHOVO

BORODINO
TSAREVO
VIAZMA

MOSCOW
VINKOVO
MALOYAROSLAVETS

GRODNO
NIEMEN

V   VII

I

X

N

II

Seeing a chance to defeat Bagration before moving north to rejoin Napoleon, Davoût (with Napoleon's permission to control Jérôme's army) informed Jérôme that he was taking command of the entire right wing. Jérôme, not told of the arrangement, flew into a rage and left for Westphalia, leaving his corps without orders and thus allowing Bagration to escape. Prepared to fight at Vitebsk, Barclay resumed his retreat upon receiving news of the extent of Davoût's advance.

Hampered by a rapidly-deteriorating supply system, the French crawled forwards while Barclay and Bagration (minus detachments) converged upon Smolensk from opposite directions. Napoleon planned an enveloping movement to turn Smolensk from the south, but by an appalling oversight forgot General Neverovsky's 9,500 Russians who bravely repulsed the French vanguard on 14 August and withdrew from Krasnyi to Smolensk in a fighting retreat. Completely losing patience, Napoleon threw his army in a bloody frontal assault against Smolensk, held by Lieut. General Raevsky's corps for two days (16/17 August) while Barclay and Bagration planned their retreat. Bagration withdrew in such haste that he forgot to cover the fords over the Dnieper so that when Barclay's turn came to leave he had to fight at Valutino and only escaped because of the slow progress of Junot (Jérôme's replacement in command of VIII Corps).

Napoleon's main army had been reduced to some 185,000 men before Smolensk, the assault on which cost about 25,000 more. Unable to gain the victory the Emperor desired, the Russians having repeatedly avoided his pincer movements, and with supply-lines already over-stretched, Napoleon should have consolidated in Smolensk and waited for spring, rather than advance on the next major objective, Moscow, 280 miles eastwards, and risk campaigning in the fierce Russian winter. Incredibly he marched towards Moscow on 25 August.

The Russian government was in chaos. Barclay and Bagration were hardly on speaking terms and many wished to oust Barclay and all other foreign staff officers in the Russian army. To resolve the disorder, the Czar was compelled to call upon a man he openly disliked – 67-years-old General Kutuzov. Fat, 'immoral and thoroughly dangerous' (according to the Czar), Kutuzov was somewhat immobile (preferring to conduct his battles from a four-wheeled 'droshky') but shrewd and greatly experienced, and regarded with great affection by the men, their esteem heightened by the fact of his being twice shot through the head with no apparent ill-effects save one blind eye (an

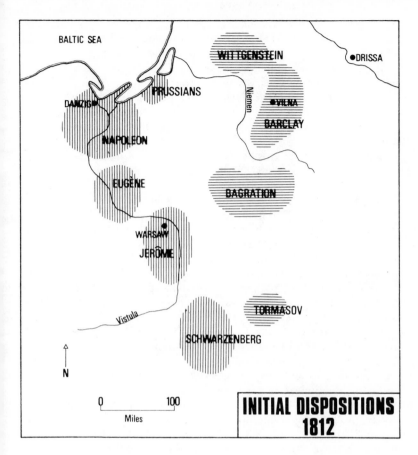

BALTIC SEA

WITTGENSTEIN

●DRISSA

Niemen

PRUSSIANS

DANZIG●

●VILNA

BARCLAY

NAPOLEON

EUGÈNE

BAGRATION

WARSAW●

JÉRÔME

Vistula

TORMASOV

SCHWARZENBERG

N

0   100
Miles

**INITIAL DISPOSITIONS
1812**

eminent surgeon who examined the scars pronounced that he was talking to a dead man)!

Kutuzov assumed command of both West armies on 20 August, with an untrustworthy Hanoverian, Bennigsen, as chief-of-staff. Joining the combined armies at Tsarevo on the 29th, he found their total strength only 100,000–120,000; though Barclay wanted to fight, Kutuzov ordered a further withdrawal to a place picked by Bennigsen – Borodino. Throughout these manoeuvres it seems that there was never a deliberate plan to lure Napoleon forwards, but simply confusion caused by lucky escapes, internal friction and (until Kutuzov arrived) uncertainty about what *could* be done. That Napoleon played into their hands was his mistake alone. Napoleon continued to advance, with Macdonald occupied on the left and Schwarzenberg and Reynier holding Tormasov and Tschitchagov on the right. With Kutuzov reinforced by only some 15,000 untried regulars and 15,000 'opolchenie' from Moscow and Smolensk ('raw peasants clutching pikes and muskets which they scarcely knew how to wield'), the immediate effective strengths of both armies were converging upon the little town of Borodino.

Kutuzov established his line on a ridge overlooking the Semyenovka creek, the line punctuated by Borodino and the Semenovskaya and Utitsa villages, with a forward position at Shevardino. Russian engineers had feverishly erected earthwork fortifications with artillery embrasures around Borodino, near Utitsa, on the right flank to cover the fords of the Kolocha River which crossed the field in a north-westerly direction, and three formidable strongpoints: the Shevardino Redoubt, the Great (or Raevsky) Redoubt and the 'Bagration flèches' (arrow-shaped earthworks), the two latter on either side of Semenovskaya. Much of the position – particularly on the left – was covered by heavy brush and woodland. Deployed behind the earthworks, Kutuzov's army had a strong right but over-extended left, only partly concealed in the Utitsa woods; both flanks were protected by cossacks and the entire front screened by light infantry. A desperate mistake by the incompetent Bennigsen was to deploy the reserves close behind the front line, which provided a perfect target for the French artillery and cost thousands of unnecessary lives.

Napoleon, with between 120,000 and 130,000 men, moved up slowly, probably intending to break through the weaker Russian left-centre, with Poniatowski's V Corps turning the left flank. Hindering deployment was the Shevardino Redoubt, held by Neverovsky's division plus Jägers and cavalry. In the early evening of 5 September, as Poniatowski swung to his left, Napoleon launched one division with supporting cavalry to take the fortification at bayonet-point. After about an hour's artillery and musket duel the French poured into the Redoubt to find it inhabited by dead, 'every living thing destroyed'. A counter-attack by the Russian 2nd Grenadier Division drove the French out again and a confused battle continued until midnight, one French unit losing 300 men when it got lost and walked into a Russian Cuirassier division. The Russians retired to their main line when the Redoubt was deemed untenable.

Hardly a shot was fired on the following day, both sides reorganising and bringing their troops into line. Committed to give battle before Moscow was endangered, Kutuzov was prepared to wait behind his fortifications and let the French come on, possibly holding his partly-concealed left wing around Utitsa for a counter-attack. He toured the army on 6 September, encouraging and directing the completion of the earthworks, and in the late afternoon a religious procession made its way around the ranks, carrying the ikon of the Black Virgin of Smolensk, until the whole army was swept by a religious fervour which reminded one officer of what he had read of Cromwell's Ironsides. They settled down to await the French.

Marshal Davoût proposed a huge outflanking manoeuvre around the Russian left, a difficult but potentially decisive move; Napoleon, still strangely lethargic, preferred a small flank movement executed by Poniatowski's V Corps alone, with a straight frontal attack on the Russian left-centre, delivered by about 85,000 men on a mile-and-a-half front. That Napoleon decided upon a simple frontal attack on prepared positions is perhaps proof of his waning power; it condemned thousands of men to death on the following day. By this time the 'Grande Armée' numbered some 133,000, with less than 30,000 horses, all units depleted by disease and the wearying march into Russia. Kutuzov's men were fewer (about 125,000) but fresher, plus a superiority in artillery (640 to 587), but this total incorporated the 15,000 'opolchenie', 15,000 half-trained recruits and 7,000 cossacks of limited use in a stand-up fight. The two armies were evenly balanced for the most horrific battle of the era.

During the night General Raevsky ordered 'wolf-pits' to be dug in front of the 'Great' Redoubt which was to bear his name, and the French constructed batteries in readiness for an early start, only to discover when dawn broke that they had been built out of range of the Russian line! By the time the guns had been re-positioned and opened fire, it was exactly 6 a.m. The first French success was the capture of Borodino by a lightning attack, in which the Russian Guard Jägers lost half their strength in fifteen minutes. A counter-attack recaptured the town but having already lost one fine regiment to no purpose, Barclay (commanding the Russian right, Bagration the left) evacuated it and burnt the bridge over the Kolocha. Meanwhile, shot and shell struck down thousands in the packed Russian ranks, which moved not a foot; except General Lavrov, V Corps' Guards commander, who had an instant nervous breakdown.

At about 6.30 a.m. the first assault was made upon the 'Bagration flèches', while Poniatowski began his attempt to turn the Russian left. One 'flèche' was momentarily taken but the French had suffered so severely from cannon-fire in the attack that a bayonet-charge drove them out immediately, Russian Hussars pursuing them to the French lines; Davoût was unhorsed and carried away half-conscious. Poniatowski had greater success, capturing Utitsa and pressing on against weakened opposition, some Russians having been diverted to help recapture the 'flèche'. Attack followed counter-attack with little success for either side as reinforcements were hustled back to hold off Poniatowski; the Russian commander, Tuchkov, was killed at the head of the Pavlovski Grenadiers but the bitter fight went on.

The Russian 7th Grenadier Division held on alone as another attack rolled up to the 'flèches'; but as their commander General Vorontsov said, 'an hour later (they) ceased to exist'. Finally two 'flèches' fell, but before the third was overrun Bagration hit the now-disorganised French with fresh troops. In the next two hours of hopelessly confused fighting Napoleon committed some 45,000 men into a horrific hand-to-hand contest, the 'flèches' changing hands several times, and 400 French and 300 Russian guns pouring death everywhere. Still the French attacked, until even Bagration clapped his hands and cried 'bravo!' at their courage; then he too went down, shot in the leg, to be carried away and die seventeen days later. Command of the Second West Army devolved upon General Konovnitsyn (confusedly running around in his nightcap) and then the more phlegmatic Dokhturov. After five hours the Russians abandoned the 'flèches', the whole area choked with bodies.

Meanwhile, General Raevsky awaited the assault at the 18-gun 'Great Redoubt', immobilised by an accidental bayonet-wound in the leg, his troops thinly-spread around. Heavy French fire annihilated two Russian horse artillery batteries; suddenly Raevsky saw French grenadiers pouring in only fifteen yards away, carried forward by a rapid second attack after the initial advance had been repelled. Raevsky hobbled to safety as three regiments of Russian Jägers bolted, leaving the place to the French. Seeing the desperate situation, various Russian generals tried to restore order, resulting in an accidental but effective four-pronged counter-attack which drove out the sole French regiment (the 30th Line, only 268 surviving) and recovered the Redoubt, but at heavy cost – the artillery commander, Kutaisov, forgetting his importance, had personally led a bayonet-charge and

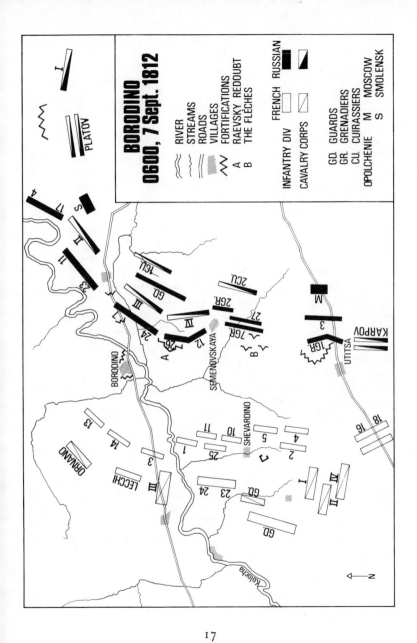

BORODINO
0600, 7 Sept. 1812

RIVER
STREAMS
ROADS
VILLAGES
FORTIFICATIONS
A RAEVSKY REDOUBT
B THE FLÈCHES

FRENCH RUSSIAN

INFANTRY DIV

CAVALRY CORPS

GD. GUARDS
GR. GRENADIERS
CU. CUIRASSIERS
OPOLCHENIE M MOSCOW S SMOLENSK

N

was never seen again; consequently much of the Russian reserve artillery was never committed – a desperate mistake.

Grouchy's III Cavalry Corps was thrown into the cauldron of fire, compelling the Russian infantry to form square; foiled, the French withdrew and increased the artillery bombardment until it seemed that the Russian divisions would be totally destroyed, but the Redoubt still held.

Whilst the attacks were going in on the Redoubt and the 'flèches', Napoleon attacked the Russian line between them. The half-demolished village of Semenovskaya was obliterated by preliminary cannonade and IV Cavalry Corps charged through heavy fire and rode over the Russian 2nd Combined Grenadier Division before it could form square, but was repelled by Russian cavalry on the other side, they in turn being cut to pieces by fresh Westphalians. South of the village I Cavalry Corps had less success, foundering on the squares of the Russian guards, who at one point actually bayonet-charged the cavalry! In the village, the Russian grenadiers picked themselves up and fought so well that only the presence of Murat himself prevented a French withdrawal. A renewed assault finally forced the Russians back, and for a time Kutuzov's army was split; but Napoleon, still lethargic and pedestrian, refused to risk his reserves to make the breakthrough. The Russians plugged the gap, and though the 'flèches' and Semenovskaya were lost, the line was intact, Napoleon again having missed the chance to end the war at one blow. Still the French artillery cut down thousands of immobile Russian infantry, who simply died where they stood.

On the Russian right, Kutuzov planned a cavalry sweep to hit the 'Grande Armée' in the rear, executed by Uvarov's regulars and Platov's cossacks, 8,000 in all. They moved hesitantly and despite minor successes retired to their original position. This lack of success was initially deplored by the Russian commanders, but actually it threw the French rear into a panic, as the cry 'cossacks' invariably did, and tied-up vast numbers of troops badly-needed in the centre. This vital move was the only thing Kutuzov did all day; he probably realized that Barclay and Bagration were competent to conduct the immediate battle themselves.

Murat's cavalry was ordered to sit unmoving for three hours, despite the temporary gap in the Russian line, under continual bombardment which caused immense losses, including the commander of II Cavalry Corps, General Montbrun, exclaiming 'Good shot!' as he fell from the saddle, mortally wounded by a shell-splinter. The Great Redoubt was pounded into a shapeless mass by the fire of 170 guns, and at last the cavalry was ordered to advance; directed by Napoleon's Aide, General Caulaincourt, II and IV Cavalry Corps outdistanced the supporting infantry and threw themselves on the shattered entrenchment. Taking a last salvo they overran the breastworks, Saxons and Poles first. Caulaincourt was killed before the fight inside the Redoubt had begun, but when it finished the Russians had been thrown out, rescuing only six of their guns. The Redoubt was heaped with dead, six or eight deep. Charging on, the French engaged the main Russian line in a ferocious two-hour cavalry battle, in which Barclay himself was twice almost killed, the artillery of both sides constantly hurling shot and canister into the combatants.

At five o'clock the battle abated, as if both sides had exhausted themselves. The Russian line had great gaps along it, but still Napoleon dared not commit his reserve, the Imperial Guard. Only on the Russian left was fierce action still progressing, with Poniatowski gradually forcing Baggovut – commander after Tuchkov's death – to give ground. A suicidal counter-attack served only to destroy two depleted Russian regiments.

The Russian army was shattered, one of its commanders mortally wounded and Barclay needing constant rum to stay on his feet; but Kutozov, far from the actual fighting, announced that he had won a resounding victory. A quick survey showed the true state of the army: Raevsky's entire corps was down to 700 men, and Kutuzov's A.D.C. Toll mistook the 2nd Division for part of a single battalion. With only 45,000 men left, Kutuzov retired, the remainder of his army straggling behind or lying on the field. The 'Grande Armée' could not pursue, for they too were decimated, exhausted and mentally shocked, and also pulled back – and Napoleon claimed a victory.

Casualty-figures for Borodino cannot be accurately assessed; about 44,000 Russians and between 30,000 and 50,000 of the 'Grande Armée' had fallen, roughly 35 and up to 40 per cent of the respective totals. Twenty-three Russian generals and 203 French staff and senior officers were casualties, and regimental figures of the units heavily engaged were worse: the Russian 6th Jägers had lost 910 other ranks, whilst the Ismailovski Guards had 435 dead. Borodino is today seen as a Russian victory, or at least a draw, in the light of later events; but at the time it appeared a French victory. Kutuzov continued to withdraw and announced on 13 September that he would not fight again before

Moscow, and abandoned it to the enemy, 'for the loss of Moscow does not signify the loss of Russia, and I see my first duty as the preservation of the army'. The news had a dismal effect abroad: the British 'Royal Military Chronicle' ran a gloomy editorial on 'the calamity of our northern allies. It is unmanly to deceive ourselves with false hopes. The battle of Borodino, and the consequent occupation of Moscow, will be followed up by tremendous consequences. Where, indeed, will the successes of this man [Napoleon] end? . . .' and even in the hard-fought Peninsular War, Rifleman Costello recorded that his whole battalion gave a day's pay to the Russian war effort upon the news of the capture of Moscow.

Napoleon sighted Moscow on 14 September, when the civilian population was streaming eastwards, evacuated by the orders of Governor Rostopchin. The French entered the city as the last Russian troops left but had little chance to plunder and loot as they wished; perhaps begun by accident, probably started by incendiaries left by Rostopchin, the city began to burn; fanned by strong winds three-quarters of Moscow was reduced to ashes by a conflagration so strong that even four miles from the outskirts a letter could easily be read at midnight. But enough remained to quarter the 95,000 survivors of the 'Grande Armée', and Napoleon wrote to the Czar demanding surrender. There was no reply.

A change of mood came over Russia as the embers of Moscow died; hitherto the army had been fired with a patriotic determination to defend the 'Motherland' but now the peasantry took up the rising tide of revenge, making Napoleon's position even more difficult. Ranging bands of cossacks and partisans (guerrillas) cut communications, albeit temporarily, as early as 24 September. Recruits and volunteers poured to join Kutuzov until his army was back to 120,000, not including partisans, whom he realised were a valuable asset: 'it does not matter that [they] wear caps rather than shakos, or . . . are clad in peasant smocks instead of proper uniforms . . .'. To assist these bands he assigned horse artillery, Jägers, Hussars and of course cossacks; led by enterprising officers like the legendary Denis Davidov they were harrying Napoleon's outposts before the month was out. At head-quarters, Kutuzov merged the two armies into a single cohesive unit and Barclay, feeling that no place for him remained, retired on the excuse of ill-health.

Realising that he could not winter in Moscow, Napoleon planned to move south to a more hospitable area, confident of beating Kutuzov if the Russians tried to stop him. But Kutuzov acted first, surprising and cutting-up Murat's cavalry at Vinkovo, causing 2,500 casualties and taking 2,000 prisoners. Napoleon marched immediately, still hampered by vast baggage-trains, 500 cannon, swarms of camp-followers and huge stacks of booty from what remained of Moscow. On 24 October Eugène's Italians, the vanguard, were halted at Maloyaroslavets by a detachment of Kutuzov's army. A fierce eighteen-hour battle raged before Eugène captured the town. Napoleon's position was now critical: to press onwards to his envisaged winter quarters might shatter his weary army in another 'victory' like Borodino. On the 25th he rode out to reconnoitre when a troop of what appeared to be a Polish lancers escort wheeled about with the cossack war-hoop and made the Emperor and staff run for their lives, before returning to the mist whence they had come. The following day Napoleon made up his mind, issuing the order for withdrawal to Smolensk – the Retreat had begun.

Followed by cossacks and expectant vultures, the 'Grande Armée' retired over the field of Borodino, hideous from the countless thousands of unburied bodies still there after fifty-two days. As the cossacks and peasant bands grew bolder the army's weakened discipline began to crumble. On 13 November Davoût's I Corps was cut off at Vyazma by Platov and Kutuzov's advance-guard; the Corps was dragged free by reinforcements, minus 6,000 casualties and 2,500 prisoners; I Corps was in total chaos – and these had been the best-disciplined troops of all. The future looked bleak.

It looked bleaker still when news came from Napoleon's flank corps: in the north, Russian general Wittgenstein had taken Polotsk in a bloody two-day action (18–19 October), and Tschitchagov in the south had by-passed Schwarzenberg and was advancing towards Wittgenstein. All hope of wintering in Smolensk had to be abandoned; supplies were running out and on 5 November came the first snowflakes. The 'Grande Armée' was doomed.

The vanguard reached Smolensk, devoured all the supplies and left nothing for the rest. Eugène moved towards the dump at Vitebsk but Platov chased him back to Smolensk; on the same day Augereau's 2,000 men were captured en masse at Lyakhovo.

The conditions of the Retreat should not be dwelt upon. The army staggered through heavier snow, discipline declining and hunger increasing. The thermometer continued to drop until after every halt hundreds never rose again. Men fought for scraps of food, rags, flayed horseskins, anything to prolong their agony another day. As the stragglers multiplied the cossacks came down, yelling, slaying and terrorising. Hundreds died at the end of a cossack lance, thousands of hunger, cold or simply the lack of will to live. No words can convey a fraction of the horror of the Retreat as every evil manifested itself, from corpse-robbing to cannibalism. The plight of the wives, children and camp-followers cannot even be imagined. The following details of the campaign refer only to the stalwarts remaining with the colours, for the vast concourse were without direction, without hope, the prey of cossacks, predators and the vengeful peasantry who perpetrated the most appalling atrocities on the weak, often unarmed and defenceless stragglers.

Through Smolensk the army was so strung-out that the Russian advance-guard cut it in half at Krasnyi, with Eugène, Davoût and Ney on the 'wrong' side. Eugène cut his way through and Napoleon turned back to rescue Davoût, but of Ney's 9,000 there was no sign. He turned up three days later with his 'Corps' – a ragged rearguard only 800 strong. The action at Krasnyi cost Napoleon 6,000 dead, 116 guns and 20,000 prisoners, and still the cossacks hit-and-ran on the flanks. Platov delightedly reported that the enemy was fleeing in 'a manner in which no other army has ever fled . . . casting aside . . . baggage, sick and wounded . . .'. Even chief-of-staff Berthier reported that only a quarter of the survivors remained with the colours, the rest having wandered off. Napoleon pushed on towards the River Berezina with Kutuzov (80,000 strong), Wittgenstein (25,000) and Tschitchagov (30,000) still converging. The 'Grande Armée's' cavalry was all but destroyed; so-called 'Sacred Squadrons' had been organised, provisional units formed from whatever officers had horses surviving but no men to command; colonels fought as cavalry troopers and generals commanded squadrons.

Reaching the Berezina at the end of November, Napoleon found the weather still against him. Possibly the mildness of the winter rather than its severity caused the destruction of the 'Grande Armée', the unusually mild weather having caused Napoleon to stay in Moscow longer than he ought, and it now melted the ice on the Berezina, so unexpected an occurrence that the army's pontoon train had been burnt at Orsha. Napoleon was marooned on the east bank.

Two ramshackle bridges were thrown across the river and the troops began to cross, attacked on both sides by Wittgenstein and Tschitchagov. A desperate fight developed as those still under arms (including

Victor's IX Corps, brought up to cover the retreat) tried to keep the bridges open. Total panic ensued when one bridge, under artillery fire, collapsed; when the Russians arrived they found the river so choked with bodies that it could be crossed on foot. Even so thousands crossed in safety, thanks to the troops who held the Russians in ferocious fighting at Studienka, reduced in many cases by lack of ammunition to holding the line by repeated bayonet-charges. On 28 November French engineers destroyed the bridge, abandoning perhaps 10,000 stragglers on the east bank to the mercies of the weather – and the cossacks.

As the remnants lurched towards Vilna, the Russians held back – except the cossacks, forever hounding the fugitives. Napoleon left the army on 5 December to return to Paris, ostensibly to raise a new army but actually to forestall the anticipated turmoil when news of the disaster reached the capital; as early as 24 October the half-insane General Malet had attempted a coup d'état. Command of the army was transferred to Murat, who emulated the Emperor and departed, leaving the competent Eugène to end the campaign.

Plans for halting at Vilna fell apart when Russian cavalry moved in barely a day after Murat's arrival and the 'Grande Armée' set out again, minus 24,000 sick and exhausted men left in Vilna. The intrepid Ney, holding the rearguard together by force of personality, tried to keep the cossacks at bay but on 10 December almost every surviving gun and waggon had to be abandoned, Berthier reporting next day that 'every human effort is hopeless. One can only resign oneself'. Two days later Ney's 1,000 men tried to defend Kovno against Platov, but the cossacks were too numerous; Ney burnt the bridge and retired across the Niemen, the last Frenchman to leave Russia. The mighty 'Grande Armée' now consisted of about 20,000 frozen, dirty and disease-ridden fugitives, only about 1,000 of whom were under arms. There remained the covering forces of Macdonald and Schwarzenberg. The bulk of Macdonald's Corps, Prussians under Yorck, defected to the Russians even before the King of Prussia formed a new anti-French alliance; Schwarzenberg simply withdrew his troops, another defection.

Two years of campaigning remained, with Napoleon on the defensive until the invasion of France forced his abdication. In June 1812 Admiral Decrès said of the Russian campaign: 'He will not return from this war; or if he does return, it will be without his army'. Six months later Napoleon's fate had been sealed by a combination of ineffective command, the resilience of the Russian nation, and the weather. Three times have powerful armies invaded Russia, and three times the result has been disaster for their commanders; strangely, while in Moscow Napoleon read Voltaire's *History of Charles XII*, apparently learning nothing from the account of the ill-fated Swedish invasion of Russia in 1718. There was even less excuse for Hitler.

The campaign of 1812 was a catalogue of horror, from the unequalled carnage of Borodino to the ghastly scenes at the Berezina, of frostbite, disease, starvation and the cossacks. Exact casualty-figures will never be known. Figures issued by the Russian Ministry of the Interior show that apart from bodies disposed of before the frosts came, Russian peasants in the Moscow area had buried 49,574 corpses and 27,849 horses by 3 February 1813; in the Smolensk area, 71,753 and over 50,000 horses; in the Vilna region 72,205 and 4,407; around Minsk over a shorter period 18,709 and 2,764; and in Kaluga 1,027 and 5,584. Beside the Berezina were found 13,106 bodies and double that number of horses. Appalling as they are, these figures are by no means the total: to them must be added the thousands drowned, buried by the French themselves, those whose bodies were never recovered from the wolves and carrion or disposed of by Russian serfs and never recorded. And to these figures *the Russian losses have to be added*.

A few examples of regimental records (though not including the vast numbers of camp-followers) show the level of unit losses. In June the Tirailleurs of the Imperial Guard had marched jauntily across the Niemen singing their regimental song:

> 'Les tirailleurs sans souci,
> Ou sont-ils? . . . Les voici.'

On 19 December the 6th Regiment of 'carefree Tirailleurs' was down to fourteen officers and ten men. In total, the Young Guard had left Moscow some 8,000 strong; 400 arrived at Vilna. The French 7th Hussars began with 1,100 men, but at the end mustered twenty mounted men and 100 stragglers. The Saxon Gardes du Corps and Zastrow Cuirassiers *combined* had twenty officers and seven other ranks alive at the end.

And of those who did survive, many were maimed with frostbite or completely broken in health.

Ten years after the débâcle, a Prussian engineer – Major Blesson –

visited the site of the Berezina crossing. The path of the army could be traced by huge piles of equipment, shakos, weapons, scraps of cloth and, at the crossing-points, mounds of bones. At the site of the main bridge an island had formed in the middle of the river, made not of rocks and earth like ordinary islands, but of bodies and vehicles which fell off the bridge, and covered with mud and sand swept down by the current of the river. Blesson inspected the location of the second bridge; no islands of dead here, since the bodies had been swept downstream where, overlooked by the now-tranquil banks of the Berezina, 'three boggy mounds had been formed, and these we found covered with forget-me-nots . . .'.

THE COLOUR PLATES

1 a) Aide-de-Camp
  b) Trooper, Élite Company, Guides of the General Headquarters.
  c) Napoleon.

2 a) Private, Chasseurs à Pied, Imperial Guard, campaign dress.
   b) Private, Grenadiers à Pied, Imperial Guard, campaign dress.

3 a) Private, Voltigeurs, Imperial Guard, full dress.
   b) Officer, 3rd (Dutch) Grenadiers, Imperial Guard, full dress.

4 a) Trooper, Grenadiers à Cheval, Imperial Guard, campaign dress.
   b) Trooper, Chasseurs à Cheval, Imperial Guard, campaign dress.

5 a) Trumpeter, 3rd Lancers, Imperial Guard, campaign dress.
  b) 'Lieutenant-Sous-Adjutant-Major', 2nd (Dutch) Lancers,
     Imperial Guard, campaign dress.

6 a) Trumpet-Major, 2nd (Dutch) Lancers, Imperial Guard, full dress.
   b) Sergeant, 2nd Carabiniers, dismounted dress.
   c) Trooper, 10th Cuirassiers, campaign dress.

7 a) Trooper, 2nd Chasseurs à Cheval, campaign dress.
  b) Cavalry 'forager'.
  c) Trumpeter, 2nd Chasseurs à Cheval.

8 a) Trooper, 8th Hussars, campaign dress.
  b) Trooper, élite company, 9th Hussars, campaign dress.

9 a) Field officer, élite company, 8th Chevau-Légers-Lanciers.
   b) Trumpeter, élite company, 5th Chevau-Légers-Lanciers.

10 a) Officer, 9th Chevau-Légers-Lanciers.
   b) Trooper, 9th Chevau-Légers-Lanciers.

11 a) Trooper, 17th Dragoons, dismounted dress.
    b) Trooper, 30th Dragoons, campaign dress.

12 a) Lieutenant, Fusilier Company, Infantry.
b) 'Deuxième Porte-Aigle', Infantry.

13 a) 'Premier Porte-Aigle', 1st Battn, 9th Line, full dress.
   b) Sergeant-Major, Fusilier company, 4th Battn, 2nd Line, with
      battalion flag, campaign dress.

14 a) Drum-Major, 15th Light Infantry, full dress.
    b) Carabinier, 15th Light Infantry, full dress.
    c) Chasseur, 10th Light Infantry, 1812 regulation dress.

15 a) Private, Infantry, 'guard order'.
   b) Grenadier, Bataillon de Neuchâtel.
   c) Captain, Fusilier Company, Bataillon de Neuchâtel.

16 a) Chasseur, 10th Light Infantry.
   b) Vivandière.
   c) Grenadier Officer, 93rd Line.

17 a) Prince Eugène de Beauharnais, Viceroy of Italy.
   b) Aide-de-Camp to the Viceroy.

18 a) Officer, Guards of Honour, undress
   b) Trooper, 1st Dragoons.

19 a) 'Officier d'Ordonnance'.
   b) Marshal Murat.

20 a) Pioneer, 7th Line (Royal African Regt), full dress.
    b) Officer. 7th Line (Royal African Regt), service dress.

21 a) '3ème Porte-Drapeau' (Sergeant-Major, Grenadier
      Company), 6th Line, campaign dress.
   b) Warrant Officer (flag-escort), 1st Velites, full dress.

22 a) Aide-de-Camp to Poniatowski.
    b) General Prince Poniatowski.

23 a) Trooper, élite company, 2nd Lancers.
   b) Trooper, 12th Lancers.
   c) Trooper, 5th Chasseurs à Cheval.

Duchy of Warsaw

24 a) Fusilier, 9th Line Regt.
   b) Grenadier Officer, 9th Line Regt.
   c) Voltigeur sergeant, 2nd Line Regt, with regimental standard.

25 a) Grenadier, 1st Regt, Vistula Legion, campaign dress.
  b) Lieutenant, 2nd Regt, Vistula Legion, full dress, with flag.

26 a) Trumpeter, Horse Artillery.
    b) Gunner, Foot Artillery, summer.

27 a) Private, Spanish Pioneers, working dress.
   b) Grenadier, Régt de Joseph-Napoléon, full dress.
   c) Private, Spanish Pioneers, marching order.

France

28 a) Fusilier, 4th Swiss Regt.
   b) Grenadier officer, 3rd Swiss Regt.
   c) Voltigeur hornist, 3rd Swiss Regt.

29 a) Grenadier, Portuguese Legion.
   b) Voltigeur, Portuguese Legion.
   c) Fusilier, Portuguese Legion.

30 a) Voltigeur, 3rd Provisional Croatian Regt.
b) Officer, 1st Provisional Croatian Regt.

31 a) Private, Chasseur-Carabiniers, full dress.
    b) Trooper, 1st Cuirassiers.
    c) Private, Guard Grenadiers, full dress.

32 a) Officer, Leib-Chevaulegers.
b) Trooper, Prince Adam's Chevaulegers.

33 a) Private, 2nd Infantry Regt, campaign dress.
   b) Jäger.
   c) Jäger.

34 a) N.C.O., 6th Chevaulegers.
   b) Trumpeter, 4th Chevaulegers.

35 a) Officer, 11th Regt.
   b) Drummer, 6th Regt.
   c) Private, 4th Regt.

36 a) Trooper, Zastrow Cuirassiers.
   b) Trooper, Gardes du Corps, campaign dress.

37 a) Trumpeter, Chevauleger Regt Polenz, campaign dress.
    b) Trooper, Chevauleger Regt Prince Clement.

Saxony

38 a) Drummer, Regt von Rechten.
   b) Private, Regt Niesemeuschel.
   c) Officer, Regt König.

39 a) Officer, Infantry, full dress.
   b) Pioneer, Infantry; full dress.
   c) Musician, Infantry, campaign dress.

Berg

40 a) Trooper, 2nd Chevau-Légers, campaign dress.
    b) Trooper, élite company, 2nd Chevau-Légers.

41 a) Trooper, Hussars.
   b) Officer, Hussars, with standard.

42 a) Trumpeter, Chevaulegers.
    b) Trooper, Portuguese Legion Cavalry.
    c) Officer, Portuguese Legion Cavalry.

43 a) Trooper, 4th Hussars, service dress.
  b) Sutleress, 1st Hussars, service dress.

44 a) Grenadier officer, 30th (Prinz de Ligne) Regt.
   b) Fusilier officer, 48th (Simbschen) Regt, campaign dress.

45 a) Grenadier, 2nd Line, full dress.
   b) Fusilier, 3rd (2nd East Prussian) Regt, full dress.

46 a) Private, Foot Artillery.
   b) Private, Foot Artillery.
   c) Drummer, Line Foot Artillery.

47 a) 'Flanquer', Imperial Guard.
   b) Driver, Artillery Train, Imperial Guard.
   c) 'Infirmier', Service du Santé.

48 a) Marshal Ney.
    b) Infantryman, campaign dress.

49 a) Trooper, 23rd Chasseurs à Cheval.
b) 'Premier Porte-Aigle', 7th Light Infantry.
c) Cuirassier.

50 a) Trooper, Starodub Cuirassiers, service dress.
  b) Officer, Chevalier-Gardes, full dress.
  c) General Kutuzov.

51 a) N.C.O., Kinburn Dragoons.
    b) Trooper, Moscow Dragoons.

52 a) Trooper, Isum Hussars.
   b) Trooper, Elisavetgrad Hussars.
   c) Trooper, Litovski Lancers.

53 a) Trooper, Pavlograd Hussars.
  b) 'Flanker', Elisavetgrad Hussars.

54 a) Ural cossack.
    b) Cossack.
    c) Officer, 4th Ukrainian Cossacks.

55 a) Trooper, 20th Light Dragoons.
   b) Cossack (Tartar).
   c) Crimean Tartar.

56 a) Kalmuk.
   b) Bashkir.
   c) Bashkir.

57 a) Musketeer, Infantry, winter.
   b) Grenadier, Infantry, summer.
   c) Musketeer, Infantry, 1812 regulation dress, summer.

58 a) Grenadier, 1812 uniform, summer.
    b) Private, Moscow Grenadier Battn, campaign dress, with flag.

59 a) Musketeer company officer, 1812 uniform, summer.
b) Company officer, Grenadier Regt Pavlovski, full dress, 1813.
c) Grenadier, campaign dress.

60 a) Private, 36th Jägers.
   b) Jäger.
   c) N.C.O., 4th Jägers.

61 a) Private, 3rd Marines, winter.
   b) Officer, Foot Artillery.
   c) Officer, Horse Artillery.

62 a) Field Officer, Foot Artillery, full dress.
   b) Drummer, Foot Artillery, summer uniform.
   c) N.C.O., Foot Artillery, winter uniform.

63 a) Jäger, Russo-German Legion.
   b) Hussar, Russo-German Legion.
   c) Gunner, Horse Artillery, Russo-German Legion.

64 a) 'Peasant cossack'.
   b) Militiaman.
   c) Partisan (peasant militia).

ORGANISATION AND STRENGTHS

Lack of space prevents any detailed account of regimental organisation and strength, 'actual' strength being often very different from the official 'establishment'. The notes below are very basic; examples of regimental organisations are given throughout the text.

Infantry regiments comprised one or more battalions (up to five or six in the French line), classed as individual units. Each battalion was composed of several companies, often four or six, of which one or two were 'élite' companies originally containing men with special skills but in many cases by 1812 often no different from the ordinary 'battalion' or 'centre' companies save in esprit de corps. The traditional élites' were the grenadiers, originally armed with the grenade but the term in the Napoleonic Wars signified what was supposedly the bravest and most veteran company (far from universally true in practice); and the light infantry company, the most agile and best marksmen, was trained to operate as skirmishers, known as 'voltigeurs' (literally, 'vaulters'); the 'centre' companies being designated 'fusiliers'. In the French light infantry the 'centre' men were termed 'chasseurs' and the grenadiers, 'carabiniers'. On occasion regimental élite companies were detached to form a composite unit (for example the Russian Combined Grenadiers). Cavalry units, organised in squadrons and/or companies, also frequently included an élite company. The German term 'Jäger' signified a unit of riflemen or light infantry.

Two or more battalions formed a brigade, in the 'Grande Armée' usually taking its name from the brigade-commander. Two or more brigades formed a division, two or more of which formed a Corps. The Corps (in theory) was a self-sufficient army complete with cavalry, artillery and transport. Virtually all formations down to brigade level in the 'Grande Armée' contained units of different nationalities, and there also existed Corps of 'Reserve Cavalry', not attached to any infantry corps.

The French army was composed of the Imperial Guard, the veteran élite containing Polish, Dutch and Italian units as well as French, and the 'line'. Due to the geography of the French empire, many line units were 'French' in name only, for example the 14th Cuirassiers and 11th Hussars (Dutch), 8th (Polish), 9th (Hamburg) Chevau-Légers-Lanciers, 19th (part-Swiss), 28th (Tuscan) Chasseurs à

Cheval, 11th (Swiss and Piedmontese), 33rd (Dutch) Light Infantry, 111th (Piedmontese), 113th (Tuscan), 123rd–126th (Dutch) and 129th (North German) infantry regiments. Recruits were drafted in regardless of nationality: for example during the campaign 1,000 Lithuanian peasants were pressed into service, half in the Illyrian Regiment and half in the 129th Line. Attached to the French army were 'foreign corps': the Swiss Regiments, the Polish Vistula Legion, the Portuguese Legion, Spanish, Croatian and Illyrian regiments, all officially part of the French army.

The Poles from the Duchy of Warsaw provided the 'Grande Armée's' second-largest contingent after the French and were generally the most reliable allied units. The two Italian Kingdoms – Italy and Naples – provided varied troops; the Italians were experienced and performed well, particularly at Maloyaroslavets, but the Neapolitans were the worst of all, with a disgraceful desertion rate. The Germans also varied in quality, some (like the troops of Baden and Berg) being among the most distinguished; others drawn in as a result of national involvement in the Confederation of the Rhine (Westphalia, Württemburg, Bavaria, Saxony, Hesse-Darmstadt) were less enthusiastic, and the smaller states contributed tiny contingents amalgamated into the conglomerate 'Confederation Regiments'. The French did not always treat their allies with due accord; for example Lieut. von Suckow of Württemburg noted: 'When rations were distributed, each loaf, each pound of meat had to be fought for. In this respect the French always treated us as little boys. It was quite another matter on the battlefield, when Napoleon's orders had to be carried out . . .'.

The Russian forces were organised on similar lines, but included vast numbers of 'irregulars' – cossacks, Asiatic tribesmen, militia and partisans – whose organisation ranged from loose to non-existent.

Great confusion can result from the different statements of strengths given by various authorities, the 'Grande Armée' varying from 750,000 to 300,000 men according to some works! The explanation lies in the definition of what comprised the 'Grande Armée': if the garrison and support troops all over Germany are included (officially part of the army), an approximate 675,000 total is reached. The actual 'field army' which began the campaign consisted of about 448,000; deducting the Austrian VII and X Corps (support and flank forces) the strength of the main army group stands at about 360,000. Appendix I details the 'Order of Battle' but basic strengths (from Chandler's *Campaigns of Napoleon*) are given below:

Corps	No. Btns	No. Sqdns	Total strength	Guns
Imperial Guard	38 (41,000)	28 (6,200)	47,200	112
I	88 (68,600)	16 (3,400)	72,000	150
II	48 (34,300)	16 (2,800)	37,100	92
III	45 (35,700)	24 (3,500)	39,200	86
IV	54 (42,400)	20 (3,300)	45,700	116
V	33 (32,100)	20 (4,100)	36,200	70
VI	28 (23,200)	16 (1,900)	25,100	55
VII	18 (15,000)	16 (2,100)	17,100	70
VIII	18 (15,800)	12 (2,000)	17,800	34
IX	43 (31,600)	12 (1,900)	33,500	80
X	36 (30,000)	16 (2,400)	32,400	84
XI	About 50,000	4 (700)	About 50,000+	60
I Cavalry		54 (12,000)	12,000	30
II Cavalry		52 (10,400)	10,400	30
III Cavalry		50 (9,600)	9,600	30
IV Cavalry		40 (7,900)	7,900	24
Austrians	26 (26,800)	44 (7,300)	34,100	60
Artillery parks, engineers etc.			18,200	230
Reserves, garrisons etc.			157,000	

Statistics of Russian forces are also difficult to assess, approximately:

Immediately available		Reinforcements brought up later	
1st West Army	126,000	From Finland	14,000
2nd West Army	40,000	From Turkish frontier	44,000
3rd West Army	45,000	From the Crimea	5,000
27th Infantry Div.	7,500	Irregulars	90,000?
Reserve and Riga garrison	37,500		
Total	256,000	Total	153,000+

Total actually employed 409,000, but note that the number of irregulars and those from the Crimea and Caucasus can only be estimated.

In 1812 the Russian artillery comprised 44 heavy, 58 light and 22 horse batteries, organised in 27 foot and 10 reserve brigades, with single horse batteries attached to cavalry formations; usual strength was 12 guns per battery. There were also two heavy and two light batteries of the Guard (16 guns each) and two Guard horse batteries (8 guns each).

UNIFORMS OF THE RETREAT FROM MOSCOW

To determine the uniform worn by a regiment at a particular moment is never easy; to do so for 1812 is difficult as that year saw a general redesigning of the costume of several European armies. Early in the year both France and Russia issued new clothing regulations which altered the appearance of much of the army, though it should not be assumed that because a uniform was introduced on, say, 1 January 1812, it would automatically be worn from that date. Firstly, the new style would usually only be adopted when the old uniform wore out, for simple economic reasons, and secondly the change could be delayed for months as it was often impossible to send the new uniform to units spread over vast areas of territory, or to have them made locally. Consequently the 'Bardin regulations' issued for the French army in January 1812 (named after their designer, Major Bardin) were in some cases not even in use by late 1813, whilst (if 'eye-witness' sources like the Elberfeld Manuscript are to be believed) in 1814 some Russian units still wore head-dress officially replaced in January 1812. Because one member of a unit is known to have worn a certain uniform it is incorrect to assume that all his fellows did likewise, as the system of sending drafts of men to existing units often resulted in more than one pattern being worn even within the same company.

It is only half-correct to describe anything as '1812-pattern', as uniforms were not produced by the same factory. Often local tailors with limited knowledge produced garments from the scant written instructions available, consequently achieving their own interpretation of the official pattern. In some cases regimental commanders deliberately ignored the regulations, many designing their own uniforms (particularly true of the Staff, Murat for example) and regimental musicians were often dressed according to the colonel's whim. Added to that are the modifications necessitated by the rigours of campaigning, regiments forced to adopt non-regulation items because of shortages of material, and items adopted on a 'personal' level, the impedimenta carried by every soldier in addition to his issued equipment, and often the use of any item available – looted civilian garments, clothing stripped off corpses, captured from the enemy or looted from an ally – to replace regulation items worn-out or lost. Thus the myriad details shown by contemporary artists which do not agree with other sources can never be judged definitely 'right' or 'wrong'; even the most unusual costume featured in an 'eye-witness' sketch could be correct; unless there is known evidence for doubting the artist's accuracy.

The above is especially true about the 1812 campaign, for once the Retreat began everything was pressed into service to prevent the individual from freezing. If the uniforms were modified, worn and patched when the army reached Moscow, they resembled a moving rag-bag as the Retreat progressed. Men trudged along wearing as many as four greatcoats, with pieces of fur tied around their bodies, clothes stuffed with rags for warmth, wearing looted petticoats, fur stoles, peasant clothing, curtains, carpets, horse-blankets, wolf-skins, shawls, pieces of flayed horse-skin, fur hats and muffs.

Major Labaume of IV Corps recorded the dress at the beginning of the Retreat 'as protection against the onslaughts of the weather . . . thus one saw walking about the camp soldiers dressed in Tartar, Cossack or Chinese style. One wore a Polish cap, another the tall hat of the Persians . . . in short, our army looked like a carnival . . . our retreat began with a masquerade and finished with a funeral'. Later, Colonel Griois of the French artillery described the 'phantoms in carnival masks' who made up the army, such pieces of uniforms as survived being covered by warmer garments, the greatcoat often 'transformed into a hooded mantle fastened round the waist with a cord'; some wore women's cloaks of valuable fur, originally a present for wife or sweet-heart. 'Nothing was more commonplace than to see a soldier, his face dark and repellent, wrapped in a coat of pink or blue satin trimmed with swan or blue fox which camp-fires had scorched and splashes of grease had soiled'. Head-gear consisted of dirty handkerchiefs tucked under the remnants of helmet or forage-cap, and feet were wrapped in ragged bits of cloth or fur. This applied not only to the rank and file: 'most of the officers, colonels and generals wore equally ridiculous and miserable costumes'.

In attempting to portray the uniforms as they actually appeared on campaign, a large number of contemporary illustrations have been consulted (some showing regulation dress) and many eye-witness accounts have been used, mentioned in the text to the appropriate plates. Many artists are quoted in the bibliography, but two deserve special mention: Christian G. von Faber du Faur, officer of the Württemburg artillery, who sketched scenes of the campaign from life (including the Retreat) and later published them as lithographs; and Albrecht Adam, a professional artist employed in the 'topographical bureau' of Eugène's Italian contingent, who departed prior to the

Retreat. In addition to the contemporary illustrations, the more modern ones consulted are those either knowingly based upon specified contemporary material, or are the work of the few genuine 'authorities' (e.g. Knötel and the Bucquoy series).

It should be noted that in many cases only generalisations can be made, there being insufficient space in which to mention the many frequently conflicting details given by contemporary sources.

1. FRANCE: a) Aide-de-Camp.
b) Trooper, Élite Company, Guides of the General Headquarters.
c) Napoleon.

The elaborate French staff uniform changed as the weather became colder until hardly any 'uniformity' remained. Napoleon's costume illustrated is taken from a Benigni drawing and a contemporary engraving by Lameau and Misbach. Numerous descriptions of his fur-lined winter greatcoat and fur cap are recorded; Butkevicius, a Lithuanian priest, saw Napoleon in early December wearing his favourite Guard Chasseur à Cheval uniform beneath a short, ermine-lined jacket, with an ermine cap lined in green velvet. In the previous month Grenadier Pils described the same cap and a fur-lined greatcoat, Marshal Berthier on this occasion wearing an identical costume but in purple; General van Hogendorp noted Berthier's incongruous appearance, 'his small frame weighed down with heavy clothing'. Other staff officers retained their 'regulation' dress with the addition of furs, cloaks, etc. (see Plate 48); for example, Baron Bacler d'Albe noted in October that he wore his uniform of Director of the Topographical Dept but with fur linings, an 'antique' riding-cloak, fur half-boots and 'my Paris cap covered with miniver'; his son, A.D.C. to General de Ségur, was 'equally well-off with a good wolf's-fur'.

General J. D. Compans wrote to his wife in mid-November describing the uniform which had given him the nickname of 'Compans the Tartar': a crimson velvet cap edged with sable, a full-dress coat minus epaulettes and embroidery, blue breeches, 'top boots' and over all a 'roomy greatcoat lined with very good fox-fur and trimmed with sable tails' extending from ears to ankles. His only indication of rank were the three embroidered stars on his sword-knot, the gold-embroidered crimson velvet sword-belt being worn over his coat.

Aides-de-camps wore a variety of uniforms, sometimes a) uniforms designed by themselves, modifying extant patterns; b) the distinctive pattern used by the immediate staff officers of a particular marshal, several marshals dressing their staff in a unique uniform so that it was instantly recognisable to which staff the A.D.C. belonged; c) regimental uniform (for those A.D.C.'s temporarily detached from their regiment for staff duties); or d) the regulation 'staff' uniform, as illustrated. Even the 'regulation' uniform frequently contained different features, either distinctions of rank or personal taste; as early as September Count Morand's A.D.C., Col. Parguez, wrote describing how he intended to line his greatcoat with fur, wear bearskin boots with the fur inwards and was contemplating the manufacture of a muff to protect his nose!

Lieut. Paul de Bourgoing, General Delaborde's A.D.C., began the campaign wearing the uniform of the 5th Tirailleurs of the Guard with white breeches, blue greatcoat, and either his Tirailleur shako with a line of embroidered stars around the top or a bicorn hat, and carrying an infantry sabre; during the Retreat this smart uniform had degenerated into a fox-fur pelisse, barrelled sash, large cavalry boots, a black silk cap worn under his hat and the sword hanging from a black leather shoulder-belt; his horse-furniture was that of an ordinary dragoon. Two further A.D.C. uniforms are illustrated in Plates 17 and 19; see also Plates 8/9 and 71, *Uniforms of the Napoleonic Wars*.

The trooper of the Guides of the General Headquarters (after Benigni) wears a dragoon-style uniform; the shabraque had a red grenade badge in the rear corners and the rolled cloak positioned at the rear of the saddle was white with a red lining. The rectangular shabraque with two holster-caps is the same shape as that illustrated in the Benigni drawing of Napoleon mentioned above, but his was of crimson cloth with heavy gold lace edging and fringe.

2. **FRANCE: a) Chasseur à Pied, Imperial Guard, campaign dress.**
   b) Grenadier à Pied, Imperial Guard, campaign dress.

The uniforms illustrated are taken from 'eye-witness' drawings by Charlet and Adam, showing the campaign dress of the 'Old Guard' in 1812. Both wear the greatcoat over the coatee (a common practice), with epaulettes worn on the coat, and loose trousers with gaiters underneath, though Adam also shows the trousers tucked into the almost-knee-length black gaiters. Both wear regulation equipment with a black oilskin cover over the cartridge-box, plus the impedimenta always accumulated on campaign – water-flasks of various patterns (the French army had no 'issue' canteens), spare boots, firewood, etc. The Grenadier's bearskin is covered with oilskin and minus plume (often tied to the sword-scabbard by the cap-cords); the Chasseur carries his bearskin in a ticken bag fastened to the top of the haversack and wears the comfortable bicorn hat divested of all decorations. Charlet also shows the bearskin worn with a cover like that of the grenadier. To judge from contemporary illustrations, the method of carrying the musket over the shoulder, held by the muzzle, was most common.

A drawing of September 1812 by Faber du Faur shows a grenadier in 'campaign' dress, the bearskin uncovered but still minus the plume and cords, the cartridge-box uncovered to show the brass eagle and four grenade badges, and the trouser-bottoms rolled up several inches to expose the ankles of the white summer gaiters. The greatcoat is worn with skirts fastened back to allow freer movement of the legs. See also Plates 49/50, *Uniforms of Waterloo* and Plate 64, *Uniforms of the Napoleonic Wars*.

Long kept in reserve, the four 'Old Guard' regiments were required to hold together the survivors during the later stages of the Retreat, which they accomplished with great distinction but horrific losses:

Regimental strengths	10 October	25 December
1st Grenadiers	1,346 men	369 men
2nd Grenadiers	1,117	234
1st Chasseurs	1,504	435
2nd Chasseurs	1,324	257

By 1 February 1813 only 408 Grenadiers and 415 Chasseurs were fit to take the field again, 'in the best uniforms available'.

3. **FRANCE: a) Private, Voltigeurs, Imperial Guard, full dress.**
   b) Officer, 3rd (Dutch) Grenadiers, Imperial Guard, full dress.

The 1st, 4th, 5th and 6th Voltigeurs present in the campaign were newly-raised or created from the old Tirailleur-Chasseurs and Conscript-Chasseurs (1810–11). Their uniform (until 1813) was of light infantry style with blue pointed-ended lapels, three pointed pocket-flaps and yellow or 'chamois' collars. Turnback-badges were green hunting-horns; cartridge-boxes initially bore brass crowned eagle badges, an order of 1813 mentioning brass hunting-horns costing 50 centimes each. A similar uniform is shown by C.-F. Weiland, but minus the shako-cords (officially removed in 1813), with a plain yellow collar, red sword-knot and round-topped gaiters minus tassel. Officers wore a long-tailed coatee with white lapels, blue collar, red pointed cuffs and gold epaulettes, and shakos with an upper band of gold oak-leaf embroidery and gold cords. Other sources show plumes of the same height as illustrated (after Weiland) but green with a small red upper section and green ball-pompom underneath. Blue breeches were popular on campaign.

The 3rd Grenadiers were raised as the Grenadiers of the Dutch Royal Guard in 1806, becoming the 2nd Grenadiers of the Imperial Guard in September 1810 and the 3rd in May 1811. Their dress was like that of the French grenadiers but white with crimson facings and (for officers) silver gorget and belt-plate with gilt eagle devices, gold-embroidered eagle on the cockade, and crimson silk woven into the gold lace of the epaulette. The rear of the bearskin had a crimson cloth patch with an embroidered gold bursting grenade; turnback-badges consisted of the same device.

The 'Young Guard' (of which the Voltigeurs formed part) was engaged throughout the campaign until the 6th Regt, for example, consisted of only 12 officers and 8 men under arms by the end of December. On 10 July the 3rd Grenadiers had a strength of 38 officers and 1,074 men; by 10 October this was reduced to 39 officers and 714 men (308 'gone astray' in the rear), and by Christmas Day only 24 officers and 17 men were left. With no hope of reconstitution, the unit was disbanded in February 1813.

The other 'Young' and 'Middle' Guard infantry participating in the campaign were the 1st, 4th, 5th and 6th Tirailleurs (similarly-uniformed to the Voltigeurs but with red plume and shako-cords and blue-piped red collar), the Fusilier-Chasseurs (dressed like the Chasseurs à Pied with Voltigeur shakos which originally carried the plume on the left-hand side), and the Fusilier-Grenadiers (uniformed like the Grenadiers à Pied but with red-plumed shako with white lace chevron on the side, and epaulettes either all-white with red 'crescent' or white with red strap; contemporary sources present conflicting evidence). Adam sketched the Tirailleurs before Smolensk, wearing loose trousers and linen shako-covers (including one on the pompom which replaced the plume on active service), with uncovered cartridge-boxes revealing the brass eagle badge.

Unlike the majority, the morale of the Imperial Guard held them together and maintained their high standard of discipline throughout the Retreat, epitomised by a letter of Lieut. Charles Faré of the Grenadiers: '. . . life is a blessing, and we have learned through resignation and hope, if not how to be happy, at least how to eat horse meat with relish!'

4. FRANCE: a) Trooper, Grenadiers à Cheval, Imperial Guard, campaign dress.

b) Trooper, Chasseurs à Cheval, Imperial Guard, campaign dress.

The Grenadier à Cheval wears the white riding-overcoat and cape with blue collar and edging, red lining, and 'aurore' tasselled lace, commonly worn over the plain, single-breasted blue 'surtout' with grey overalls, though probably the officers at least began the campaign in their full dress resembling that of the Grenadiers à Pied. The bearskin, minus cords and plume, was decorated only by the chin-scales and rear patch.

The Chasseurs à Cheval of the Guard were Napoleon's personal bodyguard, invariably forming his escort and with three distinct styles of uniform: green dolman with red facings and orange lace worn with or without the scarlet pelisse, the pelisse worn as a jacket without the dolman, and the 'petit tenue' of dark green tail-coat and red waistcoat. The man illustrated wears the dolman, green sash with red barrels, and green overalls in place of the breeches and boots; officers had a similar dress with gold lace. Over the dolman is worn the short cape, and the sabretache is plain black leather with brass badge. The busby (divested of plume, bag and cords on campaign) could be enclosed in a black waterproof cover.

The chasseur wears a handkerchief tied around the busby as a protection against the cold, this style being described by Chasseur J. M. Merme whose especial task was to light the Emperor's fire at each halt. On one occasion, as Merme was preparing the fire, wearing a handkerchief in this manner, Napoleon approached so Merme tried to remove it to appear correctly dressed. Seeing him struggling with the knot, Napoleon said: 'We are not at the Carrousel [Paris] here. It is colder today than usual, so keep the handkerchief on your head.'

Other Guard cavalry units in the campaign were the Dragoons, the Élite Gendarmes, and one company of mamelukes; see Plates 46 and 48, *Uniforms of Waterloo*, and Plates 16 and 27, *Uniforms of the Napoleonic Wars*. By February 1813 only 260 Chasseurs, 120 Dragoons and 127 Grenadiers à Cheval were fit to take the field again.

5. FRANCE: a) Trumpeter, 3rd Lancers, Imperial Guard, campaign dress.
b) 'Lieutenant-Sous-Adjutant-Major', 2nd (Dutch) Lancers, Imperial Guard, campaign dress.

There were originally two regiments of Guard lancers, the 1st (Polish) (originally the 'Chevau-Légers Polonais' created in 1806) and the 2nd (Dutch) raised in September 1810. Both wore a traditional Polish uniform of square-topped 'czapka' (lancer-cap) with 'sunburst' plate bearing the letter N, cords and white plume, the plastroned 'kurtka' (lancer-jacket) with pointed cuffs, and overalls. The 1st wore dark blue with crimson facings, piping, trouser-stripes and czapka-tops and white lace, and the 2nd scarlet 'kurtka' and

overalls with dark blue facings, piping, trouser-stripes and yellow lace (silver and gold respectively for officers). Both wore epaulette and aiguillette of the colour of the lace, the position indicating the wearer's rank.

The officer of the 2nd illustrated (taken from pictures by Lejeune and Benigni) wears campaign dress including the covered czapka, lapels fastened over to conceal the coloured plastron, and blue 'service' overalls, those of the other ranks being similar but with red lace and brass buttons. The regiment had a 'tenue de route' ('marching order') consisting of double-breasted, tail-less light blue jacket with scarlet collar and devoid of lace, worn with covered czapka and fawn overalls.

A third regiment of lancers was created at Vilna on 5 July 1812 from Polish volunteers aged between 18 and 20 and of good family who could provide their own equipment, command being given to General Konopka. Their uniform was like that of the 1st Lancers but with gold lace. On 12 September the regiment was reported ready for service, though 500 of the 1,200 horses bought by Konopka were diverted to the 1st Lancers (the only regiment at this time equipped with rough horseshoes for 'grip' on ice). After barely a month's service the 3rd was surprised and wiped out by a cossack force at Slonim (18 October); the surviving depot company at Grodno was incorporated into the 1st Lancers in March 1813. The trumpeter illustrated wears the plain service dress with leather-reinforced overalls, the shabraque having the corners folded back, a common practice on campaign. See Plate 47, *Uniforms of Waterloo*, and Plate 53, *Uniforms of the Napoleonic Wars*.

A further Guard light cavalry unit formed during the campaign (originally attached to the 3rd Lancers) was the Lithuanian Tartars raised under Mustapha Achmatowicz in August 1812 and wearing a semi-mameluke, semi-cossack uniform; see Plate 63, *Uniforms of the Napoleonic Wars*.

6. FRANCE: a) Trumpet-Major, 2nd (Dutch) Lancers, Imperial Guard, full dress.
    b) Sergeant, 2nd Carabiniers, dismounted dress.
    c) Trooper, 10th Cuirassiers, campaign dress.

The trumpet-major of the 2nd Guard Lancers wore the spectacular white uniform illustrated (after Benigni), with scarlet facings and piping, with extra gold lace indicative of rank and the white busby instead of the white-topped czapka with scarlet piping, gold cords and red-topped white plume worn by the ordinary trumpeters, whose trumpet-banners had only two tassels instead of the trumpet-major's four. In service dress the trumpeters wore sky-blue uniforms with scarlet facings and piping. White full dress uniforms were also worn by the trumpeters and officers of the 1st (Polish) Lancers, with crimson facings, piping and overalls, silver lace, and white czapka-tops.

The cuirassier's uniform includes adaptations for campaign: the full dress plume removed, 'drab' overalls and the flowing horsehair helmet-mane braided into a 'rope'. Regiments were distinguished by the facing-colours borne on the collar, cuffs, cuff-flaps and turnbacks (which had blue or occasionally white grenade badges); the following facings were worn by the regiments in the campaign:

Regt	Collar & Turnbacks	Cuffs	Cuff-flaps
1	red	red	red
2	red	red	blue
3	red	bleu	red
4	light orange	light orange	light orange
5	light orange	light orange	blue
6	light orange	blue	light orange
7	yellow	yellow	yellow
8	yellow	yellow	blue
9	yellow	blue	yellow
10	pink	pink	pink
11	pink	pink	blue
12	pink	blue	pink
14	carmine	carmine	blue

The 14th Regt was formed from the 2nd Dutch Cuirassiers originally wearing similar uniforms of white with dark blue facings. Officers wore silver epaulettes and turnback-badges and more ornate helmets and cuirasses. Sergeant Thirion of the 2nd described how he adapted his equipment; after his horse collapsed he reduced the weight to be carried by throwing away his cuirass and sabre and set out on foot armed with a double-barrelled shotgun bought in Moscow and carrying the regimental standard furled in a morocco sheath around the eagle-topped pole. Finding the weight still excessive Thirion gave the flag to the regimental colonel, the 'Eagle' to the adjutant, and burnt the pole!

Losses were so severe that by early November the four cuirassier divisions could together barely form two regiments, but were still able to execute a vital charge at the Berezina.

The Carabiniers wore similar cuirasses in brass (copper for officers) with blue cloth 'cuffs'; the figure illustrated wears gaiters instead of riding boots and no cuirass for dismounted duty. The single stripe and epaulettes with diagonally-striped scarlet and silver straps in place of the ordinary scarlet ones indicate sergeants' rank. The uniform (adopted 1810) differed in the design of cuffs: in 1812 the 1st Regt wore scarlet with white piping and white cuff-flaps piped sky-blue, and the 2nd sky-blue cuffs and flaps, both piped white. The sergeant wears the usual pouch-belt plus the waist-belt lengthened to support the sword; sword-knots were red with white

strap for the rank and file and mixed scarlet and silver for N.C.O.s. Officers had silver epaulettes.

7. FRANCE: a) Trooper, 2nd Chasseurs à Cheval, campaign dress.
b) Cavalry 'forager'.
c) Trumpeter, 2nd Chasseurs à Cheval.

The Chasseurs à Cheval wore a variety of uniforms, the 1812 regulation dress being issued in 1813 or in very limited quantity before. Jackets were either the single-breasted 'surtout' or the lapelled 'habit', both short-tailed, though it seems that some officers had longer-tailed garments than those of their men, this style not being universal – the Swebach picture entitled 'Départ de Chasseurs à Cheval' shows officers wearing the short-tailed jacket, for example. Overalls were worn on active service though breeches and boots were also used. Head-dress consisted of the shako (sometimes with red lace bands and chevrons for élite companies, who also wore epaulettes), though the busby remained popular for these companies as well as officers. The unusual arrangement of shako-cords worn by the trooper illustrated is taken directly from the Swebach picture, apparently the plaited cords hanging on the right side of the cap only. Shako-pompoms were usually in the following colours: 1st Sqdn red, 2nd sky-blue, 3rd orange and 4th violet. The white lambskin shabraques used by the rank and file were edged in the facing-colour (usually black lambskin for trumpeters), officers having dark green shabraques with silver lace; their uniforms also had silver epaulettes and distinctions.

Chasseur à Cheval regiments had dark green jackets and overalls, with the regimental facing-colour borne on the collar, cuffs, shoulder-straps, trouser-stripes and piping on the 'surtout' and lapels of the 'habit'; the fashion for green collars to be piped in the facing-colour and vice-versa was not universal. Trumpeters wore the usual variety of colours and lace. Facing-colours of the units engaged in the Russian campaign were:

describing how his full dress sabretache bore four N's ('Napoleon'), with which he confused 'a simple German' who enquired what they meant: 'Nur Nicht Nach Norden' replied Henckens, freely translated as 'Don't send us to the North'. A mere lieutenant, he commanded the remnants of his regiment at the end of the Retreat, having modified his uniform by slitting his trousers to enable him of 'perform natural functions' with minimum danger of frostbite!

The third figure illustrated shows a member of a 'foraging party' wearing a riding-greatcoat and cape with covered shako, and equipped with a scythe to collect his regiment's fodder, based partly upon a drawing to September 1812 by Albrecht Adam.

Regt	Collar	Cuffs and Turnbacks
1	scarlet	scarlet
2	green	scarlet
3	scarlet	scarlet
4	yellow	yellow
6	yellow	yellow
7	pink	pink
8	green	pink
9	pink	pink
11	green	crimson
12	crimson	crimson
16	sky-blue	sky-blue
19	light orange	light orange
20	green	light orange
23	green	dark orange
24	dark orange	dark orange
25	madder-red	madder-red
28	'amaranth'	'amaranth'

Some officers at least wore items of full dress at the outset, Lieut. J. L. Henckens of the 6th Chasseurs

See Plates 56/57, *Uniforms of Waterloo*, and Plate 43, *Uniforms of the Napoleonic Wars*.

**8. FRANCE: a) Trooper, 8th Hussars, campaign dress.
b) Trooper, élite company, 9th Hussars, campaign dress.**

Hussars on campaign commonly wore the pelisse as a jacket, or slung over one shoulder with the dolman underneath. Leather-strapped overalls were usual, though some (principally officers) would retain the breeches and 'Hessian' boots. Waterproof shako-covers and plain sabretaches with simple metal devices were other features of modified 'campaign' uniforms. Officers' dress was similar to that of the rank and file, but with metallic lace and braid. Individual details of the prescribed shako varied from regiment to regiment, some retaining the older diamond-shaped plate and others having the newer eagle-on-shield variety; some élite companies wore the shako with red lace bands, chevrons and plume, while others wore the traditional busby. The trooper of the 9th illustrated wears the 'élite' shako with the later pattern of plate, and otherwise 'regulation' uniform (the pelisse often omitted in summer); an illustration by 'Job' shows this uniform with light blue overalls with yellow piping.

Apparently at least two regiments in the 1812 campaign wore the 'rouleau' cylindrical shako (generally introduced in 1813–14) for the Bucquoy series and Knötel show the 6th and 8th Hussars wearing this pattern in Russia, both of red cloth (Knötel shows the 8th with black cords; their élite company wore busbies with cords of mixed red-and-black, red bags and red-tipped black plumes). The 8th probably began the year in shakos of the ordinary pattern, red with black leather binding and a 'tricolor' cockade on the front in place of a plate, adopting the cylindrical pattern later in the year. A further regimental feature was the mixed red-and-green or red-and-black braid; the sabretache was of plain black leather bearing a white metal 8.

Regimental colourings of the regiments engaged in the campaign are listed briefly below, but different sources are at variance in certain details:

Regt	Dolman	Collar	Cuffs	Pelisse	Breeches	Buttons and Braid
5	sky-blue	sky-blue	white	white	sky-blue	yellow
6	red	red	red	blue	blue	yellow
7	green	red	red	green	red	yellow
8	green	red	red	green	red	white buttons
9	red	sky-blue	sky-blue	sky-blue	sky-blue	yellow
11	blue	red	red	blue	blue	yellow

Though sources conflict, shako-plumes (when worn) were probably black for the 7th, 8th and 11th, black with red tip for the 6th, black with white tip for the 9th and white for the 5th. Pompoms were coloured like those of the Chasseurs à Cheval (Plate 7). Barrelled sashes were red-and-yellow for all except the 8th (red-and-green or red-and-white) and 11th (red-and-white with a blue line in the centre of the white). Pelisses usually had black fur and white lining (white and red respectively for the 11th). Overalls were coloured as the breeches except for the above-mentioned and the 7th, who had green.

Officers' cloth shabraques were coloured as the dolman, with metallic lace trim; other ranks had white sheepskins usually with a 'wolf-tooth' edging (red for the 8th and green for the 9th); the 8th had red valises with black lace and numeral, and the 9th green with yellow lace and numeral.

See also Plate 59, *Uniforms of Waterloo*, and Plate 7, *Uniforms of the Napoleonic Wars*.

9. FRANCE: a) Field officer, élite company, 8th Chevau-Légers-Lanciers.
b) Trumpeter, élite company, 5th Chevau-Légers-Lanciers.

Nine regiments of Chevau-Légers-Lanciers were formed in 1811 by the conversion of the 1st, 3rd, 8th, 9th, 10th and 29th Dragoons, the two regiments of Vistula Legion Lancers, and the 30th Chasseurs à Cheval. Their rôle was as light cavalry armed with lances, acting as scouts and skirmishers for the heavy cavalry divisions. In some cases the new uniforms were issued only at the beginning of 1812 (when the men had been trained to use lances) at which time it appears that élite companies were formed.

The first six ('French') regiments wore the brass dragoon helmet fitted with black caterpillar crest, dark green, lapelled, short-tailed jacket with pointed cuffs, shoulder-straps (epaulettes for élite companies) and dark green leather-reinforced overalls (breeches and boots may also have been worn on campaign). Regimental facings were borne on the collar, cuffs, turnbacks (with green eagle badges, and grenades for élites), lapels (which could fasten over as in Plate 5), and shoulder-strap piping; facing-colours were scarlet for the 1st, 2nd light orange, 3rd pink, 4th crimson, 5th sky-blue, 6th madder-red. Grey overalls and the single-breasted 'surtout' were also worn on campaign. Trumpeters had multi-coloured dress and often coloured helmet-crests, though the 'reversed colours' rule was not universal, some wearing 'Imperial livery' (green with green-and-yellow lace) and the first two regiments apparently dark blue with regimental facings. Officers had metallic lace and leopardskin helmet-turbans. See also Plates 56/57, *Uniforms of Waterloo*.

The 7th and 8th ('Polish') Regiments wore a dress similar to that of the Vistula Legion, typical lancer uniform of blue with yellow facings, the 8th having blue collar piped yellow. Czapkas had either yellow or blue tops (the exact date of the change in colour is uncertain), with neither cords nor plate (though one source shows a white metal 8 on the black leather band). The uniform illustrated is taken from a Carle Vernet plate, executed in 1812 and entitled 'Chevau-Léger Lancier Polonais', obviously after the change in the title but before the change in uniform, the valise still bearing the numeral 2, the number of the 8th when part of the Vistula Legion; the only apparent difference being the removal of the white metal Maltese cross (the insignia of Polish units) from the cockade. At a later date a more 'regulation' French uniform (including czapka-plate and cords) was introduced. The élite company's red-over-white plume was later changed to plain red. The gold-and-silver lace 'darts' on the thighs (indicative of rank) and the short boots are also worthy of note.

10. FRANCE: a) Officer, 9th Chevau-Légers-Lanciers.
b) Trooper, 9th Chevau-Légers-Lanciers, undress.

On 3 February 1811 the formation in Hamburg of a regiment of Chasseurs à Cheval was authorised, from members of the old Hanoverian Legion, the local dragoons and new recruits, principally German. They were allotted the number 30 but armed with lances and for a period

termed 'Chasseur-lanciers'. Shortages of material meant that a variety of uniforms were manufactured. Czapkas originally had black lower sections, no lace or plate, and red top (ultimately black with white piping but apparently retained by officers), the 'sunburst' plate being added later. Plumes were green with a 'chamois' tip, or possibly black with green tip, one source showing white cords.

There being insufficient green chasseur cloth available (and that of poor quality), a large quantity of red (originally destined for the Hamburg dragoons) was pressed into service so that the uniform issued was a strange mixture: green kurtka with 'chamois' collar, cuffs, lapels, turnbacks and piping, red trousers with black stripe, and French equipment. Shabraques were red, edged with black lace (Knötel shows a black numeral 30 in the rear corners), and valises red with black lace and perhaps numbers. Officers apparently had green shabraques with wide chamois edging, this edging piped silver on both sides. Officers wore the same kurtka with silver epaulettes and voluminous green overalls (shown by Suhr); they also wore black bicorns with white plumes.

In June 1811 the regiment became the 9th Chevau-Légers-Lanciers, but continued to wear their old uniform, being recorded by their nickname 'the red lancers of Hamburg' during the 1812 campaign. Though eventually equipped with blue Chevau-Légers-Lanciers uniform, the Elberfeld Manuscript illustrates an officer wearing red pantaloons. The trooper illustrated wears the original czapka and the greyish, tail-less 'stable jacket' with the facing-colour borne only on the collar. The lance has the original 'chamois' pennon, the white-over-red variety not being issued until 1813–14.

Trumpeters wore a laced czapka, red kurtka with black facings, white lace and epaulettes, with overalls and shabraques like the other ranks. A Leliepvre illustration shows a different uniform: black fur busby with brass chinscales, yellow kurtka with dark blue collar, lapels, cuffs and turnbacks, white lace edging to the collar and lapels, white epaulettes, scarlet breeches with white lace stripe and 'darts' on the thighs, and black 'Hessian' boots with white lace edging.

See also Plate 58, *Uniforms of the Napoleonic Wars*.

11. FRANCE: a) Trooper, 17th Dragoons, dismounted dress.
b) Trooper, 30th Dragoons, campaign dress.

The 1812 regulations prescribing a new Dragoon uniform not having been universally adopted, the majority probably wore the 'old' uniform until 1813. Both the earlier long-tailed 'habit' and the new, short-tailed jacket are illustrated, both of the traditional dragoon green. The helmet-plume was coloured in a number of regimental variations but was omitted on service. Officers wore silver epaulettes, buttons and em-broidered grenades on the turnbacks, gilt-embossed helmets and gold sword-knots; the latter were white for the rank and file and mixed red-and-white for N.C.O.s. Overalls with leather reinforcing were common for mounted duty. Élite companies, some pioneers and trumpeters had previously worn fur grenadier caps of varied pattern, probably discontinued by 1812 but possibly retained in some cases. Trumpeters had worn elaborate uniforms, usually following the 're-versed colours' scheme (the body of the coat in the regimental facing-colour) with regimental variations, white helmet-manes and aigrettes and multi-coloured plumes. The 1812 regulations introduced 'Imperial Livery' but probably many retained their old uniforms.

Originally mounted infantry, dra-goons were sometimes used in a dismounted rôle, with infantry equip-ment. Overalls and riding-boots were sometimes used for dismounted duty, but often breeches and long gaiters instead. The trooper illustrated also wears a cartridge-box over one shoulder and white cloak rolled over the other; officers' cloaks were green. The 30th Dragoon has two shoulder-belts, one supporting the pouch and one fitted with a spring-clip to secure the carbine.

In 1812 the 7th, 23rd, 28th and 30th Dragoons formed the 6th Heavy Cavalry Brigade of III Cavalry Corps, and a 'regiment' was made up of one company from each of the 2nd, 5th, 12th, 13th, 14th, 17th, 19th and 20th Dragoons, attached to the 34th Infantry Division. The facing-colours of these units were:

Regt	Lapels and Turnbacks	Collar	Cuffs	Cuff-flaps	Pockets
2	scarlet	green	scarlet	green	horizontal
5	scarlet	green	scarlet	green	vertical
7	carmine	carmine	carmine	carmine	horizontal
12	carmine	carmine	green	carmine	vertical
13	pink	pink	pink	pink	horizontal
14	pink	green	pink	pink	horizontal
17	pink	green	pink	green	vertical
19	yellow	yellow	yellow	yellow	horizontal
20	yellow	green	yellow	green	horizontal
23	yellow	green	green	green	vertical
28	orange	orange	orange	orange	vertical
30	orange	orange	green	orange	vertical

Green collars were piped in the facing colour, and vice-versa; the green shoulder-straps and pockets were piped in the facing-colour, and possibly some élite companies retained their red epaulettes and perhaps the 19th their white ones. Shabraques were rectangular, edged with white lace (silver lace and regimental piping for officers); troopers had white sheepskins trimmed in the regimental colour. Badges in the rear corners were white numerals for troopers and silver grenades for officers. Valises and officers' holster-caps were coloured like the shabraque with similar trim. However, contemporary pictures show many regimental variations to the above. See also Plate 55, *Uniforms of Waterloo*.

12. FRANCE: a) Lieutenant, Fusilier Company, Infantry.
b) 'Deuxième Porte-Aigle', Infantry.

This plate illustrates the 1812 pattern uniform introduced by the 'Bardin' regulations, which replaced the style shown in Plate 13. Its use was restricted in the 1812 campaign, one theory limiting it to I Corps. The shako, designed in 1810 and issued in limited quantities in 1811, was slightly lower and wider-topped than the 1806 model it superseded, and had a new plate consisting of an Imperial eagle on a semi-circular plaque bearing the regimental number, but regimental variations existed and it was not impossible to find the new plate on old-pattern shakos and vice-versa; officers had gold lace and gilt shako-fittings. Above the 'tri-color' cockade was a flat cloth disc, green-edged for the battalion's 1st company, 2nd sky-blue, 3rd orange-yellow and 4th violet, though again variations existed: for example, some 1st Battalions had discs of solid colour. Cords were not officially worn on the new cap but sometimes were. Usually the shako had a linen or oilskin cover on campaign.

The 1812-pattern jacket had white closed lapels and was coloured similarly for all units; turnbacks generally blue crowned N's for fusiliers (gold for officers), red grenades for grenadiers and yellow hunting-horns for voltigeurs. Grenadiers had red epaulettes, shako-trim and pompom; and voltigeurs green and/or yellow epaulettes and pompom, yellow collars and shako-trim. Either breeches and gaiters or loose trousers were worn; equipment remained the same as before with hide knapsack, white belts, black cartridge-box and the short sabre carried by (usually) grenadiers, voltigeurs, and some N.C.O.s. However, numerous regimental variations existed.

Officers' rank was indicated by gold lace epaulettes: Colonel, two with heavy fringes; Major, as Colonel but with silver straps; 'Chief de Bataillon', as Colonel but fringe on the left only; Captain as the previous but with thin fringe; Capt. Adjutant-Major as Captain but fringe on the right only; Lieutenant, as Captain but a red stripe along the strap; Sub-Lieutenant as Lieut. but with two red stripes. N.C.O.s wore diagonal stripes, two gold ones for Quartermasters, one for sergeants and two orange for corporals, all set on a red background.

In 1808 a system for providing the 'Eagle' (regimental standard) with an extra guard was initiated, the officer carrying the 'Eagle' being designated 'Premier Porte-Aigle' and two senior N.C.O.s 'Deuxième' and 'Troisième Porte-Aigles'. They were usually equipped with a brace of pistols and a half-pike bearing a small pennon, red for the 'Deuxième' and white for the 'Troisième', lettered NAPOLEON on one side and with the regimental

number on the other. Variations existed but it is known that some of this type were carried in Russia.

The figure illustrated is taken from a Carle Vernet plate illustrating the 1812 uniform, and shows an unusual carabinier-style helmet. A sabre and double pistol-holster with black bearskin cover is worn on a black waistbelt, with a narrow shoulder-belt for support; it seems possible that this dress was worn by the 'Eagle-guards' of several units in the 1812 campaign. The single-breasted 'surtout' was very popular with officers on active service; its pattern is illustrated in Plate 15. See also Plate 61, *Uniforms of Waterloo*.

13. FRANCE: a) Lieutenant 'Premier Porte-Aigle', 1st Btn, 9th Line, full dress.
b) Sergeant-Major, Fusilier company, 4th Btn, 2nd Line, with battalion flag, campaign dress.

The plate shows the infantry uniform prior to the adoption of the 1812 regulation dress. The Lieutenant of the 9th has a uniform worn in 1809, which probably remained unchanged until about 1813. The shako bears the diamond-shaped plate with regimental number cut out; the open-lapelled coatee had gold bursting grenade turnback-badges and red-piped turnbacks and pocket-flaps. As 'Premier Porte-Aigle' the officer wears gauntlets and the eagle-belt, the design of which varied, in this case having two gold lace lines and a small gilt chain-and-pickers ornament.

The 'Eagle' itself formed the regimental rallying-point, symbolising the attachment of the regiment to Napoleon and regarded almost as a holy relic. The flag illustrated is of 1804 pattern, the white diamond flanked by alternate triangles of red and blue, the white bordered by gold-embroidered leaves, and each triangle bearing the regimental number within a laurel-wreath and ribbon. The lettering on the diamond read L'EMPEREUR/DES FRANÇAIS/AU 9ème RÉGIMENT/D'INFANTERIE/DE LIGNE on one side, and VALEUR/ET DISCIPLINE/1er BATAILLON on the other. Atop the pole was the gilt-sculptured 'Eagle' on a plinth bearing the regimental number. In 1809 the 9th's 'Deuxième' and 'Troisième Porte-Aigles' were grenadier sergeants wearing black bearskin caps with brass plate, red plume and white cords, red epaulettes with gold 'crescents' and carrying a pistol in a holster on a narrow black leather shoulder-belt, and a halberd.

The sergeant-major wears the 1810 shako with coloured 'company' disc and diamond-shaped plate (worn until 1813), in this case bearing an Imperial eagle over the regimental number. The coatee has rank-stripes and service-chevrons worn higher on the sleeve. Loose trousers, commonly worn on campaign, were made of linen or canvas, coloured from white, ochre, brown to grey and could be tied at the ankle; gaiters were worn underneath.

Battalion flags used as 'markers' and rallying-points were not held in esteem like the 'Eagles'; those of the 9th had silver-painted lettering and pike-heads of a uniform 'spear' shape. The design varied, those of the battalions engaged in Russia being: 1st, a red flag with a horizontal blue stripe at top and bottom edges; 2nd, a blue flag with similar red stripes; 3rd, three red and two blue alternate horizontal stripes of equal width; 4th, a red and blue vertical bar (one source shows the blue section nearest the staff); and 6th, two blue and one red alternate horizontal stripes. The lettering was placed near the edges but on the blue stripes of the 3rd's flag and at the edges of the blue segment of the 2nd's. The upper line of lettering read 2me RÉGt. DE LIGNE and the lower 1er, 2me BATAIL-LON, etc. The flags of the 3rd and 6th Btns had red 'cravats' (streamers) bearing a gold crowned eagle, and a single mixed red-and-gold tassel. Each battalion flag was carried by a sergeant-major and escorted by two 'Fourriers' (senior N.C.O.s) whose rank-badge was a single gold stripe, edged red, on the upper arm. The flags were stored in the regimental transport during the Retreat and captured by the Russians.

14. **FRANCE: a) Drum-Major, 15th Light Infantry, full dress.**
    b) Carabinier, 15th Light Infantry, full dress.

c) Chasseur, 10th Light Infantry, 1812 regulation uniform.

The Light Infantry wore a mixture of 'old' uniforms (characterised by the coatee-lapels ending in a point at the lower edge) and those prescribed by the 1812 regulations. The chasseurs ('centre' companies), carabiniers ('grenadiers') and voltigeurs comprising each battalion were usually distinguished as follows:

CHASSEURS: red collar piped white, green epaulettes with red 'crescents' or shoulder-straps, white hunting-horns on the turnbacks, white shako-cords and green plume in full dress.

CARABINIERS: as chasseurs, but red grenades on the turnbacks, red epaulettes and shako-plume.

VOLTIGEURS: yellow collar (often piped red), white or yellow hunting-horn turnback-badges, epaulettes of combinations of yellow, green and sometimes red, yellow or green shako-cords and green and/or yellow plume; occasionally wore busbies in full dress.

As the 'prestige' branch of the infantry the light regiments deliberately maintained regimental patterns and distinctions. Some carabiniers wore the bearskin cap in full dress as illustrated (after the Carl Collection). Shako-ornaments were generally like those of the line but of white metal, with varied designs of lacing and shako-plate. Officers had silver epaulettes and distinctions.

The 1812 pattern uniform resembled that of the line but with blue lapels. The uniform of the 10th illustrated (after Boisselier) shows the unusual 'tricolor' cockade instead of a plate. Musicians of light infantry wore colourful and at times exotic uniforms, that of the 15th's drum-major illustrated (in the uniform of 1809) providing an example. The pioneers of this regiment wore a similar dress (plus the usual apron, belts, gauntlets and axe common to all pioneers) but with a black busby with red bag and plume, white piping and cords. However, contemporary sources often conflict. See also Plate 63, *Uniforms of Waterloo*.

15. FRANCE: a) Private, Infantry, 'guard order'.
b) Grenadier, Bataillon de Neuchâtel.
c) Captain, Fusilier Coy, Bataillon de Neuchâtel.

The unusual infantry private's uniform is taken from a Faber du Faur drawing of early October 1812, showing a man on guard duty, wrapped up against the cold in a privately-acquired fur-lined cap and muff, a scarf and a dressing-gown worn underneath the greatcoat. The musket-lock and muzzle are also wrapped.

The Bataillon de Neuchâtel was a Swiss unit raised in 1807, engaged in Spain from January 1810 until despatched in March 1812 to join the 'Grande Armée'. By October the regiment (including companies of artillery, engineers and artillery-train) was in Smolensk. The Retreat caused severe loss: from the original 1,027 only thirteen officers and seven men regained the regimental depot at Besançon. The battalion was reconstituted from recruits, fought through the 1813–14 campaigns and was one of the last to surrender, defending Besançon for eleven days after Napoleon's abdication in 1814.

The Bataillon de Neuchâtel wore infantry uniform of the unusual 'chamois' colour, with red facings. The exact shade of yellow is uncertain (it would vary with every batch of uniforms received) but was not the brilliant tone shown by some modern works, though of sufficiently bright a yellowish-beige to prompt the regimental nickname, 'canaries'. The dress probably worn at the beginning of 1812 is illustrated, though possibly prior to the campaign the 'habit-veste' with pointed cuffs was adopted. The brilliant yellow piping on the officer's collar was repeated on the lapels of the full dress coatee (the illustration shows the 'surtout' frequently worn on active service). Fusiliers wore the French infantry shako with white metal eagle plate, 'tricolor' cockade, white cords and ball-tuft, white epaulettes and five-pointed chamois stars on the turnbacks; grenadiers in full dress wore the bearskin cap (devoid of decoration), otherwise the shako with red ornaments, red epaulettes, chamois grenades on the turnbacks and red sword-knots; voltigeurs had green shako-cords and plumes, green epaulettes with yellow 'crescents', green sword-knots and green hunting-horn turnback-badges. The white breeches were worn with white gaiters in summer, and loose trousers on campaign; one illustration shows a voltigeur's gaiters shaped like those illustrated but with green lace edging and tassel.

The officer wears a cloth shako-cover with the silver cords removed. Drummers may have worn 'Imperial Livery' but one source shows a blue jacket with red facings. The artillery detachment wore blue jackets with yellow facings and piping, artillery shako and blue breeches; the train had the same with steel-grey cuffs; and the engineers blue jackets with black collar and cuffs, yellow lapels and red piping. See also Plates 56/57. *Uniforms of the Napoleonic Wars.*

16. FRANCE: a) Chasseur, 10th Light Infantry.
b) Vivandière.
c) Grenadier officer, 93rd Line.

The chasseur of the 10th Light Infantry wears a shako-cover with a flap which could be let down as a neck-guard, and has a red cloth patch on the greatcoat-collar; he wears the summer gaiters and trousers and the cartridge-box bore a brass hunting-horn badge.

A very considerable number of women accompanied the 'Grande Armée' into Russia. Each unit had its 'vivandières', ladies employed as sutleresses to sell food, alcohol, tobacco, etc. to the members of the regiment, frequently accompanying their unit into action where it was not unknown for them to become casualties whilst tending the wounded.

They often wore 'uniforms' resembling that of their regiment and usually with features of their own design; the braided jacket and shortish skirt worn over breeches and gaiters were typical, as was the 'round hat', frequently decorated with long, coloured scarves (that illustrated taken from Faber du Faur). A universal item was the barrel worn on a shoulder-strap, often gaily painted with regimental devices, with attached measuring-beaker and cup, from which alcohol could be sold on the march. In addition to the 'official' vivandières, a vast concourse trailed after the army, soldiers' wives, officers' ladies, and the genuine 'camp followers' of dubious occupation. One French officer (in the Peninsular War) said that whereas the British had an army, the French had a 'walking brothel'. The plight of these women and their considerable number of children on the Retreat from Moscow can scarcely be imagined.

The officer of the 93rd is taken from a picture by Christoph and Cornelius Suhr, a drawing-master and his brother who produced a remarkable album of pictures (commonly known as the *Bourgeois de Hambourg* book) depicting the uniforms of troops passing through Hamburg between 1806 and 1815. These 'eye-witness' sketches often contain unusual features of modified 'campaign' dress; identification and precise dating is often difficult but that illustrated is identified as the 93rd Line *c.*1812–13 by Dr Paul Martin in his *Der Bunte Rock*. The grenadier cap (officially replaced by the shako) is retained by

two officers in Suhr's picture, one having a plate bearing the Imperial eagle. The coatee has a number of unusual features and bears the ribbon of the Légion d'Honneur. One officer has a gorget with (apparently) the usual eagle badge, the other having a plain gilt version. Suhr also shows an officer wearing a black bicorn hat with gold loop and silver lace pompom, and one in a shako ornamented with gold lace and diamond-shaped plate.

17. KINGDOM OF ITALY:
a) Prince Eugène de Beauharnais, Viceroy of Italy.
b) Aide-de-Camp to the Viceroy.

Eugène de Beauharnais, son of the Empress Josephine by her first marriage, was appointed Viceroy to Napoleon as King of Italy in June 1805, in which capacity he commanded IV Corps and ultimately the remnants of the army.

The uniform shown – worn in May/June 1812 – is taken from a drawing by Adam, resembling a French Marshal's dress in pattern, the Orders being the Légion d'Honneur and the Grand Cross of the Order of St. Etienne of Hungary.

The A.D.C. illustrated, in 'service' uniform, comes from a painting by General Lejeune. Adam shows an ornate dress consisting of the same hat, long-tailed dark green coatee with cut-open, light-infantry lapels, sky-blue collar, cuffs, and piping on lapels and turnbacks, white piping around the pointed cuffs, silver epaulettes (the left one fringed), a silver-braided sky-blue waistcoat, dark green breeches with silver stripe and Austrian knots on the thighs, and Hessian boots with silver lace and tassel. The horse-furniture was like Eugène's, but with a single silver lace band around the edges.

18. KINGDOM OF ITALY:
a) Officer, Guards of Honour, undress.
b) Trooper, 1st Dragoons.

The Italian Dragoons wore French-style uniforms, the 1st (Queen's) Regiment which participated in the Russian campaign having pink facings; riding-boots were worn for mounted duty. Contemporary sources conflict in minor details; the brass helmets had leopardskin turbans (after Leinhart & Humbert) but some illustrations show black fur as used by the 2nd Dragoons. The shoulder-straps were piped in the facing-colour, though brass scales may have been worn. Green grenade badges were worn on the turnbacks (silver for officers, who had silver epaulettes); musicians wore 'reversed colours' and élite companies the bearskin cap with red plume and cords (sometimes shown with black peak and brass plate bearing a grenade) and red epaulettes. Officers had rectangular green shabraques with silver lace edging and bearing a silver crowned N in the rear corners; other ranks had white sheepskin with a 'wolf tooth' edging in the facing colour.

The Guards of Honour wore a dragoon uniform with red facings, but on campaign frequently wore the 'undress' uniform of a tail-less single-breasted jacket or a 'surtout' with silver-laced turnbacks, both plain dark green, with green or grey overalls with or without black leather reinforcing. Officers had silver collar-lace and epaulettes, sometimes worn suspended from the epaulette-button hanging on to the breast; Adam shows these with a fringe on the left and an aiguillette on the right. Cloaks were white, Adam showing an officer in a green double-breasted greatcoat with silver-edged cape and collar-lace like the jacket. The elaborate helmet had a caterpillar crest supported by a gilt comb shaped as an eagle, and bore the cypher N and the Iron Crown of Lombardy on the front-plate. Adam noted that these helmets were so large and unmanageable that they frequently fell off, so the forage-cap would be extensively used; officers had dark green caps with silver lace band and rosette on the crown with a silver tassel suspended; troopers' caps had a red band. Adam sketched a trooper evacuating wounded at Smolensk wearing the undress jacket and the full dress helmet. White breeches and high-boots were worn in full dress, and Knötel shows a trooper wearing loose white trousers with the undress uniform. Equipment was of French pattern, the pouch-badge consisting of a gilt eagle under the Iron Crown of Lombardy. See also Plates 24/25, *Uniforms of the Napoleonic Wars*.

19. KINGDOM OF NAPLES:
a) 'Officier d'Ordonnance'.
b) Marshal Murat.

Joachim Murat (1767–1815) was renowned for two characteristics: vanity and bravery. Enlisting as a trooper from penury, he rose to become Marshal, Duke of Berg and ultimately King of the Two Sicilies (Naples), and married Napoleon's sister Caroline. A fearless cavalry leader, he was a universal favourite with the French cavalry (and the cossacks!), and quite nerveless in action. His vanity proclaimed itself by his long, curled hair, cosmetics, and the outlandish uniforms he designed for himself. That illustrated is after a portrait by Gros, the peakless czapka bearing the crimson-and-white Neapolitan cockade, and the pockets of the kurtka ornamented by three tassel-ended silver lace loops. The breast stars are those of the Royal Order of the Two Sicilies and (below) the Légion d'Honneur; the sash of the Neapolitan order was worn uppermost, except in Napoleon's presence when the scarlet Légion d'Honneur ribbon was most prominent as a mark of respect. The jewel-studded golden oriental sabre is now in the Musée de l'Armée, Paris; with this uniform Murat used a shabraque made from a complete tiger-skin.

Several witnesses recounted Murat's uniform during the campaign. Albrecht Adam saw him in July – a 'striking person' in a gold-braided light blue jacket, gold-laced red trousers and 'a strange hat lavishly decked with plumes', Adam initially mistaking him for an over-dressed drum-major! Lieut. von Suc-

kow of the Württemburg Guard Jägers saw Murat wearing a 'Henri IV'-style hat with white plumes and diamond clasp, open-necked light blue velvet jacket with gold embroidery, Tudor-style ruff, gold-fringed light blue silk sash, white 'stockinet' breeches and enormous deerskin boots in Thirty Years War style, with huge gold spurs. Surgeon-Major von Roos of the 3rd Württemburg Mounted Jägers wrote of Murat's red and green Spanish cloaks and red, green or yellow Hungarian boots! In colder weather, General van Hogendorp saw Murat at Vilna, 'huddled in huge and superb furs' and an enormous fur hat, giving him the appearance of 'a walking colossus'.

Murat, alas, was no politician and was executed by firing-squad after an abortive attempt to regain his kingdom. 'I have faced death too often to fear it' he said to the firing-squad, and, vain to the last, added: 'Save my face – aim at my heart – fire!'

The 'Officier d'Ordonnance' (staff officer) is taken from a watercolour by Fort presumably showing campaign dress of 1812, minus pelisse, with a plain cocked hat and black leather sabretache bearing a crowned Imperial eagle in gilt; this badge was also borne on the gold-edged crimson pouch, suspended from a gold-laced white belt. The officer wears the silver, crimson and blue enamel medal of the Royal Order of the Two Sicilies. A Descamp painting shows a full-dress uniform, the dolman having white facings, plus gold-laced white pelisse with light brown fur, gold-laced scarlet breeches, gold-laced crimson Hussar shako with white plume, and gold-laced crimson boots. The sword-belt and slings were crimson with gold lace, and the sabretache-face crimson, bearing the same gilt eagle badge, but edged with wide gold lace and a heavy bullion fringe. The shabraque shown by Fort is entirely of leopard-skin, with a gold lace and sky-blue cloth edging.

20. KINGDOM OF NAPLES:
a) Pioneer, 7th Line (Royal African Regt), full dress.
b) Officer, 7th Line (Royal African Regt), service dress.

The Neapolitan units were one of the 'Grande Armée's' weakest links, as recognised by Napoleon in a letter to his brother Joseph (then King of Naples) in 1807, refusing to let the Neapolitans carry 'Eagles', because 'you must be aware that . . . these troops are no better than none at all . . .'. The general standard can be gathered from the fact that when the 'Pioniers Noirs' (raised in 1803 from negroes and mulattoes from Santo Domingo) were in French service they were regarded as the worst unit of the army; when transferred to Neapolitan service in August 1806, under the title of 'Royal African Regiment' (7th Line), they were superior to any existing unit of the Neapolitan forces! In 1812 the Neapolitans had one of the highest desertion-rates in the 'Grande Armée'.

Murat reorganised the Neapolitan army, including the uniforms; in 1811 a short coatee with closed lapels was issued, white with coloured facings, red epaulettes and plumes for grenadiers and green for voltigeurs, and a French-pattern shako with shield-shaped brass plate bearing the regimental number, most other details resembling those of the French army. The fur cap was worn by grenadiers and pioneers in full dress, the white cap illustrated bearing the Neapolitan cockade. The pioneer also wears the traditional gauntlets, leather apron and rank-badges in the form of two inverted chevrons over crossed axes over a bursting grenade; Knötel shows these badges all situated above the elbow. The officer (wearing service uniform) is taken from the Freyberg Manuscript (1813), which shows another figure in this uniform but with blue collar and gilt gorget. Though some of the original N.C.O.s were commissioned, many of the officers were European. The Royal Africans apparently never crossed the Russian border, but saw action in East Prussia in 1813, Sergeant Bourgogne writing of members of the unit lying dead in the snow near Elbig in January 1813.

21. KINGDOM OF NAPLES:
a) '3ème Porte-Drapeau' (Sergeant-Major, Grenadier Company), 6th Line, campaign dress.
b) Warrant Officer (flag-escort), 1st Velites, full dress.

Both figures wear the white uniform mentioned in the text to Plate 20, with the distinctive items of dress and equipment reserved for N.C.O.s attached to regimental colour-parties.

Contemporary sources present conflicting evidence of the Neapolitan Velite uniform at this period — for example some show the lace loops with tasselled ends, absence or presence of white piping to the facings, and one shows a private in campaign dress wearing flat-topped cuffs with red flaps, yellow cap-cords, plain green plume and loose buff trousers. The probable explanation is that active service resulted in the manufacture of uniforms conforming only basically to the official regulations, dependent upon the interpretation of local tailors and the availability of materials. The epaulettes worn by the Warrant Officer are shown by one source as gold, others showing various designs for the rank and file (red, green with yellow or red crescents); the two chevrons on the cuff are further indications of rank, and turnback-badges were gold grenades. The halberd and pistols were indicative of the flag-escort. Officers had gold lace and cap-cords.

The sergeant-major of the 6th Line wears grenadier uniform (other companies had shakos); facings, epaulettes and service-chevrons were all in the regimental facing-colour, 'amaranth'. The fur cap bore brass grenade plate, 'amaranth' cords and plume and Neapolitan cockade, the sword-knot was mixed white and 'amaranth', and the loose overalls were used only on campaign. The '3ème Porte-Drapeau' (to use French terminology) carried a halberd with sky-blue pennon bearing an 'amaranth' crown over conjoined cypher N and 6; that of the '2ème Porte-Drapeau' was similar but with a white background.

22. DUCHY OF WARSAW:
a) Aide-de-Camp to Poniatowski.
b) General Prince Poniatowski.

The army of the Duchy of Warsaw (as befitted an Imperial satellite) was organised on French lines but retained traditional Polish features. The Duchy provided the 'Grande Armée's' strongest contingent after the French and the highest percentage of troops compared to the total population. The Polish units contained some of the best elements of the army (none entered the war with greater enthusiasm) but rapid expansion resulted in a high porportion of recruits. During the Retreat the surviving Poles – knowledgable of the terrain and climate – proved invaluable to the evacuation of Russia.

Prince Joseph Antoine Poniatowski, commanding V Corps, epitomised the valiant Polish character and was a figurehead for Polish hopes of independence. Created a Marshal of France at the Battle of Leipsig (1813) he drowned three days later whilst trying to ford the River Elster. His uniform illustrated is based on a print published in Dresden in 1813; the kurtka has unusual decoration formed by doubling a strip of silver lace back upon itself to form a zigzag pattern. The plastron was reversible, blue or crimson, with sometimes a 'triangle' of crimson visible at the top when the blue side was worn outwards. The right epaulette had a silver aiguillette attached. The uniform's colouring and style, the czapka (with fur band), the crimson overalls and black pouch bearing silver eagle badge were all traditional Polish features. The ribbands and breast-stars are those of the Légion d'Honneur and the Polish 'Virtuti Militari' (black cross on a silver star-plate), the latter ribband worn uppermost except when in Napoleon's presence; the silver breast-star is the 'Grand Aigle' of the Légion d'Honneur.

The A.D.C. wears Polish hussars costume of the striking crimson and sky-blue colouring, with silver lace and light grey pelisse-fur. The two Polish hussar regiments — numbered 10th and 13th in the line cavalry – wore the same dress but with dark blue pelisse and dolman, faced crim-

Contemporary sources of Polish uniforms often conflict. The Lancers wore black czapkas, the white cockade with white metal Maltese Cross badge, and Polish eagle-plate with 'shield' part bearing pierced regimental number. All regiments wore dark blue kurtka and overalls; epaulettes were normally white and plumes often black (white for senior officers) but contemporary pictures show numerous exceptions. Distinctions of units engaged in Russia are shown below.

The 2nd, 3rd and 7th had yellow trouser-stripes, the 8th and 9th red and the remainder crimson. The élite trooper illustrated (after Linder) wears company distinctions of red epaulettes and fur cap, shaped like the Portuguese 'barretina', with ornaments like a busby and brass shako-

Regt	Collar and piping	Plastron and piping	Cuffs and piping
2	red/white	dark blue/yellow	red/white
3	crimson/white	dark blue/white	crimson/white
6	white/crimson	dark blue/crimson	crimson/white
7	yellow/red	dark blue/red	yellow/red
8	red	dark blue/red	yellow/red
9	red/blue	dark blue/white	dark blue/white
11	crimson/white	crimson/white	dark blue/white
12	crimson/white	dark blue/white	dark blue/white
15	crimson/white	crimson/white	crimson/white
16	crimson/white	dark blue/crimson	crimson/white

son, yellow lace for the 10th and white for the 13th.

23. **DUCHY OF WARSAW:**
  a) **Trooper, Elite Company, 2nd Lancers.**
  b) **Trooper, 12th Lancers.**
  c) **Trooper, 5th Chasseurs à Cheval.**

plate. Lance-pennons were probably red-over-white for the 2nd, 3rd and 16th, and red, dark-blue-and-white for the remainder. Other sources however show red-over-yellow or yellow-over-red pennons for the 2nd; lances painted in crimson-and-white spirals, white overalls with blue stripes (both 3rd, after Linder); pennon yellow-over-blue-over-red and yellow epaulettes with red fringe (7th, after Gembarzewski), and shabraques varied from black sheepskin over dark blue cloth to white sheepskin over a red shabraque with blue inner and yellow outer borders (2nd). Trumpeters wore more multicoloured costume.

The Chasseur à Cheval regiments were numbered 1st, 4th and 5th in the line. The dark green, French 'surtout' and overalls had coloured facings, piping and trouser-stripes (1st scarlet, 4th crimson, 5th orange). Epaulettes had brass-scaled straps and white fringes, red for élites who also wore black fur busbies with either red or green-over-red upright or drooping plumes or red ball-pompom; cords (when worn) were red. Officers had gold lace, élites with silver cap-cords and gold pompom, and field officers white plumes. Pouches were black with gilt badge of the regimental number between two sprays of foliage (shield bearing regimental number and surmounted by a grenade for élites). Dark green pointed-ended shabraques were edged in the facing colour (gold lace for officers), though white sheepskins with facing-coloured 'wolf-tooth' edging were also used. Trumpeters' uniforms usually consisted of white busby with usual decorations, white coatee with regimental facings and gold lace, cut open to reveal a braided waistcoat, and ordinary overalls. The Polish busby had no hanging 'bag' but a padded cloth top (usually of the facing colour), with pleats radiating from a central lace boss.

24. DUCHY OF WARSAW:
a) Fusilier, 9th Line Regt.
b) Grenadier officer, 9th Line Regt.
c) Voltigeur sergeant, 2nd Line Regt, with regimental standard.

The two basic styles of Polish infantry uniform were the traditional czapka and dark blue kurtka with coloured facings and piping, or French-style dress worn by the 4th, 7th and 9th Regts. French-style distinctions were red for grenadiers and mixtures of yellow, green and/or red for voltigeurs. The white Polish cockade was worn by all except those in French uniform, who had the 'tricolor'. No general rules can be given due to the large number of regimental variations.

The sergeant of the 2nd Regt has a plain czapka-plate, though some units used the Polish eagle-on-shield variety. The plume is of voltigeur colouring, fusiliers usually having a ball-tuft. Indications of rank were the gold stripe on the kurtka, gold epaulette-crescents, czapka-lace and mixed crimson-and-white cords. Sergeant-majors wore two gold stripes on the sleeves, 'fourriers' a gold v chevron on the upper arm, and corporals two yellow lace stripes. Polish flags varied as much as the uniforms (see black-and-white Plates F and G), usually consisting of an embroidered eagle over the title, in this case LEGIA. I. and PULK 2 PIEHOTY (*sic*), sometimes with silver fringe. The pike-head was a large sculpted eagle of silver with gilt crown and gilt-lettered plinth bearing the regimental title on the front and WOYSKO

POLSKIE on the reverse. Many variations of this pattern existed; for example a flag of the 4th Regt of similar design had one side sky-blue and in addition to the eagle and PULK 4 title bore an embroidered inscription translated as 'Sewn and made by the hand of Sofia Potocki wife of the first Colonel of the Regiment'. Other units carried flags originally belonging to earlier Polish corps.

The grenadier officer of the 9th wears a variation of the grenadier cap which existed in French style, with or without plates, peak and cockade, with various plumes or cords, etc. Officers also wore French-style bicorns and single-breasted 'surtout' as well as the pre-1812 'habit' illustrated.

The fusilier of the 9th wears French 1812-style jacket (though the French shako was also worn with the kurtka). A picture of the 4th shows a similar uniform but with yellow lapels and shoulder-straps and dark blue turnbacks, all piped red, and white breeches. A Chelminski illustration of the 12th at the Berezina shows the French shako worn with the ordinary grey overcoat. The 13th wore a unique all-white uniform with sky-blue facings and the usual czapka; raised from Austrian prisoners in Galicia in 1809, it is possible that Austrian uniforms were adapted to produce this striking dress. Polish regulations stated that officially fusiliers should be clean-shaven, voltigeurs should wear a moustache and grenadiers both moustache and side-whiskers. Musicians' uniforms were frequently white and ornamented like those of the French army; those of the

4th, 7th and 9th appear to have adopted 'Imperial Livery' during or after 1812.

Further examples of the varied infantry uniform are provided by the following brief descriptions:

BUGLER, 16th REGT (after Knötel): czapka as illustrated but with white-laced crimson top, yellow cords, green pompom and crimson-over-yellow plume; white kurtka with white lapels, turnbacks and cuffs and yellow collar, all piped crimson; blue trousers; brass horn with green cords.

OFFICER, 7th REGT, campaign dress: French shako with yellow oilcloth cover; dark blue 'surtout' with red collar piped white, gold epaulettes (left only fringed); white breeches; black 'Hessian' boots with black lace and tassel.

PRIVATE, 8th REGT: czapka as illustrated with white cords and green plume, plate with a white metal eagle above the 'point'; dark blue kurtka with crimson collar, cuffs and plastron, all piped white, white cuff-flaps, blue turnbacks piped crimson; dark blue trousers, white gaiters.

VOLTIGEUR, 12th REGT: black czapka with brass plate shaped like that on a French grenadier cap, green cords, green pompom and plume with yellow tip; dark blue kurtka with white plastron, yellow collar and crimson pointed cuffs, white epaulettes; long white trousers, black gaiters, green sword-knot.

25. FRANCE: a) Grenadier, 1st Regt, Vistula Legion, campaign dress.

b) Lieutenant, 2nd Regt, Vistula Legion, full dress, with flag.

The four infantry regiments of the Vistula Legion originated as the 'Légion Polacco-Italienne' of the Westphalian army, transferred to French service in March 1808, the fourth regiment raised in 1810. Apparently by 1812 all wore the French shako with brass 'sunburst' plate bearing either the letter N or the regimental number, with white cords (silver for officers with two 'raquettes' on the right-hand side), carrot-shaped red pompoms for grenadiers, probably white plumes for fusiliers and green or green-and-yellow for voltigeurs. The 1812-pattern jacket was dark blue with facings (probably): 1st Regt, blue collar, yellow cuffs; 2nd, yellow collar and cuffs; 3rd, yellow collar, blue cuffs; 4th, blue collar and cuffs (though one source shows crimson facings for the 4th); officers had silver lace. White epaulettes were probably worn only by grenadiers, fusiliers having blue shoulder-straps piped yellow, and voltigeurs green-and-yellow epaulettes. The officer illustrated – the 'Premier Porte-Aigle' of the 2nd Regt – wears a distinctive plume and the traditional Polish Maltese cross on the cockade; lieutenants' epaulettes had a red stripe on the strap, the turnback-badge consisting of a silver-crowned N. The medal is the Polish 'Virtuti Militari'.

The flag shown *may* have been carried in Russia; certainly, it was present with the regiment at Sedan in April 1812. The flag was that of the old 1st Polish Legion of the Revolutionary Wars, its design consisting of a light blue field bearing an eight-pointed white star, the four diagonal points having a red 'dart'. The central design – a cockerel with a spray of palm and laurel and a lightning bolt in its talons – was the same on both sides, the cockerel always facing away from the pole. The two light blue scrolls above and below the cockerel were lettered in gold, the upper one reading RÉPUBLIQUE FRANÇAISE, and the lower, on one side, PREMIÈRE LÉGION POLONAISE and on the other 2ème BATAILLON. In 1800 the pole was striped red, white and blue but may by 1812 have been painted dark blue.

The grenadier wears a covered shako and an unusual 'campaign' dress described by Capt. Heinrich von Brandt of the 2nd Regt. In the difficult march from Smolensk to Gzatsk, in burning heat and a strong wind stirring up enormous clouds of dust, many soldiers to protect themselves 'improvised dark spectacles out of bits of window-glass', carried the shako and wore a handkerchief over the head, with a hole torn out of the front; others garlanded themselves with leaves to prevent choking with dust. Brandt's comment that this presented 'a strange sight at times' is perhaps the understatement of the campaign!

This superb Polish corps was attached to the Imperial Guard during the campaign, initially only the first two battalions of the 1st, 2nd and 3rd Regiments; the 3rd Battalions and the entire 4th joined during the Retreat. See also Plate 48, *Uniforms of the Napoleonic Wars*.

26. DUCHY OF WARSAW:
a) Trumpeter, Horse Artillery.
b) Gunner, Foot Artillery, summer.

The Polish Foot Artillery (created December 1806) was established in March 1812 at twelve field companies and four 'static' ones. At the outset of the campaign the combined Horse and Foot Artillery totalled 104 guns and 1,500 men, but suffered so severely that only ten cannon and four howitzers survived until 1814. The Horse Artillery, raised and equipped by Count Wladimir Potocki in 1808 at his own expense, was formed into a regiment in 1810 with 690 men and 902 horses. Wrecked by the Retreat, only one battery remained when the valiant corps was re-organised at Sedan in 1814.

The Foot Artillery wore the kurtka (and the earlier French, open-lapelled 'habit') of dark green with black facings and red piping, green turnbacks piped red and red epaulettes (gold for officers). Dark green trousers and black gaiters were worn in winter, and white in summer. The French-style shako had red cords and plume and brass Polish eagle-plate. Rank-distinctions were: Colonel, two bullion-fringed epaulettes; Lieut. Col., as Colonel but no fringe on the right shoulder; Captain, two plain-fringed epaulettes; lieutenant as captain with a crimson stripe on the strap; sergeant-major, two gold stripes above the cuff; sergeant, one stripe; bombardier, two yellow stripes.

The original Horse Artillery uniform included czapka and kurtka, but from 1810 Chasseur à Cheval uniform was worn, with black busby with red cords and pompom (gold for officers), dark green single-breasted, short-tailed jackets with black collar, cuffs, and turnbacks, all piped red, and dark green overalls with black side-stripes piped red on both edges. Epaulettes had brass-scaled straps and red fringes (gold for officers, who wore gold aiguillettes); gold grenades were worn on the collar and turnbacks. Trumpeters wore more colourful uniform, two distinct styles being shown by Linder and Chelminski; that shown (dated 1810) includes a white busby of Polish style (without a bag but with a padded cloth top); another, dated 1812, shows a similar head-dress with green top with a gold boss in the centre, white jacket with black facings and turnbacks, red epaulettes, scarlet breeches with yellow stripe, and black 'Hessian' boots with gold lace.

27. FRANCE: a) Private, Spanish Pioneers, working dress.
b) Grenadier, Régiment de Joseph-Napoléon, full dress.
c) Private, Spanish Pioneers, marching order.

The two Spanish units were one of the most undistinguished contingents of the 'Grande Armée', with a high desertion-rate. The Régiment de Joseph-Napoléon was formed from ex-French auxiliary troops who had mutinied against their commanders and been imprisoned; formed on 13 February 1809 the unit was named after Napoleon's brother and consisted of four battalions, two serving in I Corps and two in IV Corps. The white French-style uniforms were faced green, the shade different in various sources, from light to 'Imperial' green. The shako (shown with grenadier distinctions) had a grey-blue cover on campaign.

The Spanish Pioneers (or Engineers) were attached to the Imperial Guard, the uniform illustrated taken from the Carl Collection. The undress cap ('bonnet de police') was used by all French units, basically a stocking-cap folded over and tucked into the head-band, the colour usually that of the regimental uniform with piping of the distinctive colour; it was carried rolled and strapped under the cartridge-box. The shako had a diamond-shaped plate with a 'tricolor' cockade above, and is shown with the chinscales fastened around the rear, a common style. The painted sign-board was used as a marker for the constructions carried out by the regiment.

28. FRANCE: a) Fusilier, 4th Swiss Regt.
b) Grenadier officer, 3rd Swiss Regt.
c) Voltigeur Hornist, 3rd Swiss Regt.

The Swiss regiments in French service were among the best troops in Europe. Long associations with France (from the Swiss Guard of the Ancien Régime to the Helvetian demi-brigades of the Republican era) led to the creation of Napoleon's first Swiss unit in July 1805, followed by three more infantry regiments in October 1806, each including an artillery company. Napoleon wrote in May 1807: '. . . the Swiss of our day, like their fathers, will appear with the same glory on the field of honour. I value their bravery, fidelity and loyalty; it is this sentiment that brings me to decide that all these regiments shall be composed only of citizens [of Switzerland] without mingling in deserters or other foreigners, for it is not the number of soldiers that makes the strength of armies but their loyalty and good faith . . .'. Serving with the 'Red Division', all four Swiss regiments won great distinction in Russia; at the Berezina they had to hold the line to enable the crossing to be made, repeatedly charging with the bayonet when their ammunition was expended. They held the line and saved their 'Eagles' but left 80 per cent of their effectives on the field: at Vilna, for example, the 3rd Regt arrived with only sixty men. 'They were, right to the end of the retreat, invincible; they outdid nature, and they spread a radiance of heroism into this desert of snow . . .' (Marshal Gouvion St. Cyr).

The Swiss corps wore French uniform of the traditional red colour (the old Helvetian demi-brigades had worn blue but were ordered in 1803 to 'revert' to red) the officers' uniforms being a true scarlet and those of the other ranks a madder shade, 'quickly taking on a shade of violet' to quote one contemporary opinion, with white linings which faded to yellow after a short time. Facings were: 1st Regt, yellow piped sky-blue; 2nd, royal blue piped yellow; 3rd, black piped white; 4th, sky-blue piped black. The red grenadier epaulettes did not show against the coats so the 2nd took blue epaulettes and the 3rd white, the latter eventually being adopted by all. The grenadier cap was officially restricted to the 1st but was probably worn by the others as well. This cap is shown worn by the officer of the 3rd; officers had gold lace and crowned eagles on the turnbacks, and some contemporary pictures show the officers of this regiment wearing black gloves to match the facings. The undress 'surtout' was dark blue.

The voltigeur hornist of the 3rd wears the 1812-pattern jacket with the 'old' diamond-shaped shako-plate. In 1812 Carle Vernet showed voltigeurs wearing fusilier shako with yellow pompom, 'chamois' collar and shoulder-straps, piped red, no piping on the cuffs or lapels, and white cuff-flaps piped red. One contemporary painting shows the 3rd's Voltigeur officers armed with the 'Versailles' carbine, and equipped (apparently) with a cartridge-box worn as a belt over the left shoulder, bearing shield-shaped plate and two 'pickers' attached by two small chains to an eagle-boss higher on the belt.

The fusilier of the 4th also wears the 1812-pattern uniform, the shako-plate like that on the grenadier cap; dark blue piping is shown by some sources instead of the black author-ised; a dark blue crowned N was worn on the turnbacks. For some time the Swiss wore the earlier pattern shako with plume and cockade on the left, with cords, but in 1812 the later pattern was apparently universal. The 1st Regt clung to the blue coats of the Helvetian demi-brigades long after the 'official' introduction of red, and even in 1811 their officers wore the older silver epaulettes and buttons. Probably the white N.C.O. chevrons had become yellow by 1812 but there is no conclusive evidence.

29. FRANCE: a) Grenadier, Portuguese Legion.
b) Voltigeur, Portuguese Legion.
c) Fusilier, Portuguese Legion.

The Portuguese Legion was formed from Portuguese nationals in January 1808 with a strength of six infantry and two cavalry regiments (establish-ment of May 1808), re-organised in May 1811 into three infantry and one cavalry regiment (see also Plate 42). Heavily engaged in Russia (including an attack on the bridge at Smolensk, where they charged the Russian 30th and 48th Jägers), the Legion lost so heavily that it was disbanded in 1813. Ludwig Schlosser, a resident clergy-man near Leipsig, recorded them behaving 'much better than the French did . . . co-operative and good-natured . . .'; far from removing or eating everything in sight as did the rapacious French, the Portuguese even offered to share their rations with Schlosser, that being the custom with their own priests in Portugal! Faber du Faur's sketches, however, show them laden with looted provisions, geese and goats, and the Hessian Captain Franz Roeder accused them of committing 'the grossest excesses', maltreating civilians, women and children and generally behaving in a barbaric manner, though many crimes committed by French troops were also blamed upon them.

Contemporary sources show differing details for the Legion's uniform, perhaps indicating regimental features within the Legion. The distinctive and characteristically-Portuguese brown jacket had red facings, white piping and either white or red turnbacks. The Portuguese 'barretina' shako had red cords for grenadiers, green for voltigeurs and probably white for fusiliers, with plumes red, yellow-over-red and white respectively, though variations are found. Grenadiers had red epaulettes, voltigeurs green with red or yellow 'crescents', and fusiliers wore brown shoulder-straps; officers had silver epaulettes and lace, brown breeches and knee-boots and (like the French) black bicorns as an alternative to the shako. Drummers are shown in ordinary uniforms with silver loops on breast and cuffs, silver hoops on the sleeves, silver-laced collar and silver-edged red epaulettes with mixed red-and-silver fringe (though one source suggests dark green jacket faced red); drums were brass with light blue hoops.

The fusilier wears a pointed-topped shako-plate like that used by the Portuguese army, bearing the regimental number (and perhaps a grenade and hunting-horn for grenadiers and voltigeurs), with a crown above; contemporary sources show the chinscales fastened at either front or rear of the cap, Faber du Faur in one picture apparently showing large cockades behind the chinscale-bosses. The loose trousers and the jacket-design (with cuff-flaps) are also taken from Faber du Faur. The trousers had been worn for full dress earlier in the Legion's history, laced red; the removal of the shako-cords and plume were concessions to active service. The grenadier (after the Carl Collection) has an unusual (and perhaps apocryphal) shako-plate of a crowned shield; the jacket has shorter lapels and pointed cuffs. The breeches and gaiters are from Faber du Faur, though white breeches are also shown in contemporary illustrations. The voltigeur (from a Moltzheim sketch, after Horace Vernet) wears the voltigeur plume and epaulettes but shako-plate and cords indicative of the grenadiers. This unusual combination may be explained by the fact that on campaign, whatever was available was used by whoever could acquire it! The beard – normally reserved for pioneers in most European armies – perhaps supports the theory that the original was based upon a 'campaign' sketch. The jacket-lapels in this case are shown closed to the waist.

30. FRANCE: a) Voltigeur, 3rd Provisional Croatian Regiment.

b) Officer, 1st Provisional Croatian Regiment.

The Peace of Vienna (1809) ceded the Croatian frontier to France, this area being geographically divided into six 'regiments', the inhabitants of each forming two military battalions, one administrative and one irregular battalion and numerous other departments, from which in 1811 two Provisional Regiments (of two battalions each) were raised for service with the 'Grande Armée'. The first-raised was the 3rd Provisional Regiment, from the 1st Btn of the 5th Croatian Regiment (1st Banat) and the 1st Btn of the 6th (2nd Banat); the 3rd Provisional served throughout the Russian campaign with great courage, only 17 officers and 141 men out of almost 2,000 remaining fit and under arms on 30 December 1812. The 1st Provisional Regiment was formed from the 1st Btns of the 1st (Lika) and 2nd (Ottochaz) Regiments; over 1,700 men marched from Trieste to join IV Corps, in which they served with distinction. The regimental colonel, Slivarich, was promoted General but only 53 survivors reached the safety of Königsburg.

Both regiments wore dark green French light infantry dress with yellow facings and piping, the 3rd having a light blue collar-patch; long trousers with yellow stripe on the outer seam are shown worn by all companies. Grenadiers had red epaulettes, shako-lace and plume; one source shows an officer of the 3rd with a shako-plate shaped like that of the voltigeur, silver chinscales, ball-pompom and embroidered leaf-motif band around the top, a short-tailed, single-breasted 'surtout' with facings and turnbacks like the ·voltigeur, and green trousers with silver stripe. A drummer of the 3rd is shown in a light blue jacket with yellow collar and cuffs, red epaulettes, mixed red-and-white lace, a grenadier shako with red tuft, breeches like the voltigeur and red-tassled gaiters.

The 1st wore a similar costume, the officer illustrated having the 'old' diamond-shaped shako-plate. Brown or grey greatcoats were worn by this unit, with a yellow collar-patch shaped like that illustrated in Plate 16. One version of the trousers had a double yellow stripe; both white and black gaiters were worn. The cartridge-boxes of the 1st at least bore white metal Imperial eagle badges, and one source shows a black cloth shako-cover.

The 2nd Provisional Regiment was not raised until 1813; they should not be confused with the Illyrian Regiment of III Corps (which wore a blue light infantry uniform) nor with the Dalmatian Regiment of IV Corps.

31. WESTPHALIA:
   #### a) Private, Chasseur-Carabiniers, full dress.
   #### b) Trooper, 1st Cuirassiers.
   #### c) Private, Guard Grenadiers, full dress.

VIII Corps, composed of Westphalians, was initially commanded by King Jérôme Bonaparte of Westphalia, renowned only as a dissolute profligate, once even arrested for drunkenness by his own police! After he abandoned the army following friction with Napoleon, VIII Corps passed to Junot, an equally unstable character. Generally composed of good troops, the Westphalian corps was unfairly handled throughout, being given the unwelcome task of clearing the fields of both Smolensk and Borodino. It suffered appalling casualties: from its establishment strength of over 27,000, it was down to 1,700 by 9 November, 500 on 13 November and only 240 on 22 November. Only fifty infantry and sixty cavalry crossed the Berezina.

Westphalian uniforms were elaborate and of French design. The élite Chasseur-Carabiniers, recruited from foresters and gamekeepers of the Royal estates, served as light infantry armed with rifled carbines. The uniform illustrated is taken from a Sauerweid engraving; another such shows officers' dress, even more magnificent with much gold lace (including larger Austrian knots on the thighs) and heavy gold shako-cords.

The Guard Grenadiers wore white uniforms with red facings and sword-knot, based on that of the French Imperial Guard; campaign dress consisted of short, single-breasted jacket of the same colouring, French shako with diamond-shaped brass plate, red pompom and the blue-and-white Westphalian cockade; officers had gold lace.

The 1st Cuirassiers wore the red-faced white uniform until about 1812, when the coatees became dark blue; the 2nd Cuirassiers wore blue faced orange. The caterpillar-crested helmet had a white plume for full dress; equipment was of French pattern. The other cavalry consisted of the Garde du Corps (steel helmet with gilt embossing, white plume, black crest; dark blue jacket faced red; French-style cuirass with gilt 'sunburst' on the front: see Plate 44, *Uniforms of the Napoleonic Wars*); the Guard Chevau-Légers (dark green jacket faced red, yellow lace; dark green breeches laced yellow; leather helmet of French Chevau-Légers-Lanciers style with gilt fittings); and two regiments of hussars dressed in French style, the 1st wearing white metal eagle-shaped shako plate and green plume, green dolman, breeches and pelisse with black pelisse-fur and white lace, red-and-white barrelled sash and black leather equipment, and the 2nd with similar uniform but light blue dolman, pelisse and breeches with red facings, white shako-plume and grey pelisse-fur.

Infantry regiments wore French uniform, the diamond-shaped shako-plates bearing an eagle over regimental number, white coats with dark blue collar, cuffs, lapels and turnbacks, gold lace for officers; grenadiers had red shako-cords, plumes and epaulettes, voltigeurs green cords and epaulettes and yellow-tipped green plumes, and fusiliers white cords and pompom in 'company' colours (1st Company light blue, 2nd white, 3rd yellow, 4th green), and white shoulder-straps edged in the facing colour, changed in 1812 to dark blue epaulettes with white 'crescents'. The light infantry wore the shako with white metal eagle-plate and green plume, dark green coat with light blue collar, pointed cuffs, turnbacks and piping, dark green trousers or dark green breeches and black gaiters, and black leather equipment.

Some contemporary sources present conflicting information for Westphalian uniforms, and numerous non-regulation items were adopted on campaign: Major von Lossberg, for example, recorded the purchase of 'a yellow-brown beaver cloak with a double collar'.

32. WÜRTTEMBURG:
a) Officer, Leib-Chevaulegers.
b) Trooper, Prince Adam's Chevaulegers.

The Württemburg contribution to the Confederation of the Rhine forces for the campaign amounted to some 14,000 men (plus 1,800 reinforcements), serving in III Corps; though unenthusiastic about the war they fought with distinction but suffered severely; as early as August their effective strength was down to 4,000, and on 10 November Napoleon remarked on the remnant of the Württemburg contingent still marching in formation – about thirty strong.

The cavalry regiments were numbered from 1 to 5 (the 5th, Dragoons, did not participate in the campaign). The two Chevauleger regiments (1st Prince Adam's and 2nd Leib-Regiment) wore a similar uniform, with large black leather helmet bearing yellow-and-red cockade on the left, and helmet-plate usually consisting of crowned cypher over the motto 'Furchtlos und Treu' (the Royal Arms for officers), and yellow-over-black crest; dark blue jacket faced yellow

for the 1st and red for the 2nd, and wide facing-coloured girdle for the rank and file. The lapels were edged with facing-coloured piping and the yellow turnbacks bore a blue line for the 1st and red for the 2nd. Leinhart and Humbert mention that the Leib-Regiment's élite company was known as the Life-Squadron and wore bearskin caps. Shabraques were small, dark blue edged with facing-coloured lace, and bearing crowned FR cypher in the rear corners; other ranks had white sheepskins with facing-coloured 'wolf-tooth' edging. Officers had blue cloth shabraques with metallic lace edging, piped red inside and blue outside, with crowned cypher in front and rear corners.

The 3rd and 4th Mounted Jägers wore green uniform (including breeches) with yellow piping for the 3rd and white piping and pink collar for the 4th; both had white metal buttons and helmet-fittings, the 3rd with yellow and green caterpillar crest and the 4th all-green.

33. WÜRTTEMBURG:
a) Private, 2nd Infantry Regt, campaign dress.
b) Jägers.
c) Jägers.

The Württemburg infantry uniform illustrated is that worn after the adoption of blue lapels in 1811 (previously of the facing colour) but before the shako replaced the helmet in 1813, with the French equipment which replaced the earlier single shoulder-belt and waist-belt. The facing-colour was borne on the collar, cuffs, shoulder-straps and turnbacks, the units engaged in Russia wearing:

1st, yellow; 2nd, sky-blue; 4th, black; 6th, white; 7th, yellow. Piping was white for all except the 6th, which had red. Faber du Faur shows loose, pale-coloured trousers worn on campaign instead of the white breeches and black gaiters, absence of helmet-decorations (plume and cockade removed) and the practice of wearing a rolled blanket or greatcoat over one shoulder.

The Württemburg Jägers wore dark green 'rifle' dress, the 1st Jägers with yellow buttons and the 2nd, white. Faber du Faur shows this uniform with short lapels with two or three buttons below (as worn by most Württemburg units), and modifications for campaign: minus shako-cords, knee-boots worn outside the trousers, and sword-bayonet hanging low on the front of the left thigh from a black leather shoulder-belt. The Jägers apparently evolved an unusual system of skirmishing, shown by Faber du Faur in a drawing of the fight at Semonovsky (Borodino); fighting in pairs, one man fired his carbine whilst the second stood ready to protect his comrade with fixed sword-bayonet.

The two Württemburg Light Infantry units wore an infantry-pattern uniform of dark green with light blue facings, white piping, brass buttons and (after 1807) the shako with red pompom.

34. BAVARIA: a) N.C.O., 6th Chevaulegers.
b) Trumpeter, 4th Chevaulegers.

About one-sixth of the Grande Armée's Bavarians (most in VI Corps) were recruits from the Tyrol, where an uprising against Napoleon had been quelled shortly before, the Tyroleans consequently having little loyalty to Napoleon or Bavaria (whose troops had helped suppress the rising). The unsettled Bavarian regiments had a higher desertion rate than any other German contingent, the temperamental Corps commander, Gouvion St. Cyr, doing little to reassure them. They lost heavily in actions around Polotsk and virtually disappeared in the Retreat.

The six Chevauleger regiments in the campaign wore the distinctive leather helmet with large crest (bearskin for officers and N.C.O.s, wool for other ranks), with brass plate bearing the MK cypher, light blue and white cockade under the plume, and brass chains hanging from studs on the side of the helmet, attached to the chinscale-bosses and looped around the front, the label bearing the abbreviated title CHEVLEGERS REGI-MENT. The black leather chinstrap had brass chain edging; brass scales were also worn. The dark green jackets had regimental facings and piping, and very small badges set on the facing-coloured turnback-edging, the outer badge a lion and the inner a crown. The part of the shoulder-scales nearest the collar was cloth. Lace rank-distinctions on the collar were one, two or three stripes up to sergeant and captain, repeated with lace collar-edging for higher ranks. Officers wore fully-scaled epaulettes, scarlet-edged light blue pouch-belts with silver lace, and mixed white and light blue sashes. Trumpeters had lace-edged collars (this lace double for trumpet-majors who also had hanging sleeves). Shabraques were red, pointed-ended, edged with two gold lace stripes for officers and a single white lace stripe with interwoven light blue diamonds for other ranks, whose shabraques bore white, crowned MK cypher in the rear corners; officers had the cypher and crown, within a laurel wreath, in front and rear corners.

Facing-colours borne on lapels, cuffs, and turnback-edging were red for the 1st, 2nd (Taxis), 4th (König) and 5th (Leiningen) Regiments, and black for the 3rd (Kronprinz) and 6th (Bubenhofen). Collars were 1st and 2nd green, 3rd and 6th black with red piping, and 4th and 5th red. Buttons and lace were white for the 1st, 4th and 6th and yellow for the remainder.

Baron Chlapowski of the Polish Lancers of the Guard recorded meeting the confused Bavarian General Wrede in Vilna during the latter part of the Retreat, running around the streets and leading about fifteen soldiers with fixed bayonets. The frantic general was dressed in a civilian coat, 'a sort of turban on his head', no gloves and his face so swathed in handkerchiefs that Chlapowski could only recognise him by his voice!

35. BAVARIA: a) Officer, 11th Regt.
b) Drummer, 6th Regt.
c) Private, 4th Regt.

The Bavarian infantry wore the traditional light blue uniform and crested leather helmet ('Raupenhelm'), in the crown of which N.C.O.s kept their notebooks and other ranks their cleaning kits (in 1812 it was suggested that the mess-tin should be re-designed to fit inside the helmet!) Although not official until 1818, some helmets had a neck-flap which could be lowered. The small woollen tuft worn below the cockade on the left-hand side was restricted to fusiliers; grenadiers had taller red plumes and 'sharpshooters' green. The colour of these tufts varied but from 1811 were usually of the following colours for companies numbered one to eight: white, white/yellow, green, green/yellow, green/red, red/yellow, blue, blue/yellow.

The 'cornflower'-blue jacket had regimental facings and piping and red-lined turnbacks; officers had very wide silver sashes with interwoven light blue strands; badges of rank as for cavalry. In addition to breeches and gaiters, long white or grey trousers (light blue for officers) were introduced in 1808 and 1805 respectively, for use on campaign or fatigue dress. Musicians (after Leinhart and Humbert) wore ordinary dress with metallic lace (silver or gold according to button-colour), with 'swallow's nest' wings; some authorities give differing details for various regiments. French-style equipment had replaced the hitherto untidy Bavarian arrangement of pack and straps. Regimental details were:

Regt		Lapels and cuffs	Collar	Piping	Buttons
1	König	red	red	—	white
2	Kronprinz	red	red	—	yellow
3	Prinz Karl	red	red	white	yellow
4	Sachsen-Hildburghausen	yellow	yellow	red	white
5	Preysing	pink	pink	—	white
6	Herzog Wilhelm	red	red	white	white
7	Löwenstein-Wertheim	pink	pink	—	yellow
8	Herzog Pius	yellow	yellow	red	yellow
9	Isenburg	yellow	red	red	yellow
10	Junker	yellow	red	red	white
11	Kinkel	black	red	red	white
13		black	red	red	yellow

(The 12th had been disbanded for mutiny.) The 1st and 2nd had lace button-hole loops of white and yellow respectively.

The light infantry wore similar uniforms of dark green with black cuffs and lapels, red piping and turn-backs, with collars red for the 1st (Gedoni) and 2nd (Wrede); 3rd (Bernclau) and 4th (Theobald) black; 5th (Buttler) and 6th (La Roche) yellow. Buttons yellow for the 1st, 4th and 6th and white for the remainder. Their helmets had different tufts for companies: red, green, blue, yellow, red/black, green/black, and short red plumes for Carabiniers. Breeches and trousers were grey (green or white trousers for officers).

Although the regulations specified cuff-flaps with four buttons, some illustrations show the three-button type. Officers sometimes defied the official ruling prohibiting buttons on the outer seam of the trousers. The double-breasted greatcoat was lightish grey until January 1811 when a darker version was introduced; possibly both types were worn during the campaign. Buttons were cloth-covered, and the standing collar bore a patch with pointed rear edge, of the colour of the jacket-collar, with a button within the point; shoulder-straps grey. Officers had collar-patches of metallic lace. The rank and file had blue mittens lined with white baize.

36. SAXONY: a) Trooper, Zastrow Cuirassiers.
b) Trooper, Gardes du Corps, campaign dress.

The Gardes du Corps and Zastrow Regiments of the Saxon contingent both wore the traditional pale-coloured German heavy cavalry uniform; originally this colour represented the 'buff-coats' worn in the seventeenth century. Both corps were heavily engaged at Borodino, assaulting the Raevsky Redoubt with the utmost valour; it seems likely that the initial breach was made by the two Saxon units who charged headlong into a mass of Russians, heedless of casualties. Losing over half their strength in this fight, both regiments were virtually annihilated by the Retreat; of the 850 who had charged at Borodino only 20 officers and 7 other ranks survived to the end of the campaign, plus 48 prisoners-of-war released by the Russians.

Both wore the large crested helmet, with gilt ornamentation on the fur turban for officers; plumes were white (white-over-black for officers and black-over-white for N.C.O.s). The short-tailed jacket was white faced yellow for the Zastrow and straw-yellow with blue facings for the Gardes du Corps; the former had white lace (silver for officers) but the Gardes wore an elaborate design of yellow, blue and red (gold for officers) on the collar, cuffs, turn-backs and down the breast. Officers of both units wore laced pouch-belts and fringed epaulettes, the other ranks having metal shoulder-scales.

Both should officially have worn cuirasses, but those of the Gardes had been left in Warsaw, but as General Latour-Maubourg remarked before the charge at Borodino, these were not necessary for the regiment to maintain its fine reputation. The Zastrow wore black-enamelled cuir-ass-fronts only (the traditional German pattern), with yellow cloth 'cuffs'; the white cloak with yellow cape illustrated is taken from a contemporary illustration, much of the material for this plate coming from Sauerweid. White gauntlets and breeches were usually worn, but the uniforms in this plate have been modified as described by Lieut. R.

von Schreckenstein who charged with the Zastrow at Borodino; both units, he recorded, wore grey cloth breeches and used their 'long riding-cloaks' on campaign; at Borodino the Gardes du Corps wore the cloak in a bulky roll across the chest in lieu of the cuirass, so that 'the men were reasonably well protected'. In addition to the sword all were equipped with a carbine and two pistols.

Trumpeters of both apparently had red plumes and helmet-crests, though one source shows yellow for the Zastrow. Their trumpeters wore yellow jackets faced white, with regimental lace and probably no cuirasses; those of the Gardes had red jackets faced blue, regimental lace and a line of mixed red and white lace around the upper arm. The Gardes had a set of elegant silver trumpets with gold cords, which (like the standards of both units) were lost during the Retreat. Trumpet-cords of the Zastrow were either yellow or mixed yellow, black and white. The rectangular shabraques had rounded ends for the rank and file, yellow with two white lace lines for the Zastrow (one silver band for officers according to Sauerweid), and blue with regimental lace edging (gold for officers) for the Gardes. Holster-caps were of a similar pattern, bearing the same device as the shab-raque's rear corners: a white crowned FR cypher for the Zastrow (officers no device) and the same in red-and-yellow for the Gardes (gold for officers). Valises were blue for the Gardes and yellow with white lace for the Zastrow. Von Schreckenstein records that the Gardes du Corps had large black or brown horses, but the Zastrow smaller (though sturdy) mounts; officers' horses were of all shades.

The light-coloured uniforms were instantly recognizable on the battle-field: Berthier saw white uniforms inside the Raevsky Redoubt and exclaimed, 'The Saxon cuirassiers are inside!' Napoleon, seeing the blue jackets of the Polish and West-phalian cuirassiers in support, said that as they were dressed in blue, 'they must be *my* cuirassiers', a deliberately unfair comment as he wished the credit for the brilliant charge to go to a French unit!

See also Plate 77, *Uniforms of the Napoleonic Wars.*

37. SAXONY: a) Trumpeter, Chevauleger Regt Polenz, campaign dress.
b) Trooper, Chevauleger Regt Prince Clement.

The bulk of the Grande Armée's Saxons – over 20,000 and one of the best contingents – were in VII Corps, and as such escaped the severe losses of the Saxon units in other corps.

The four Chevauleger regiments engaged wore French-style uniform, their shako with white plume and cords and plate marked with the Royal cypher. The regiments (each of 670 men in four squadrons) wore the distinctive red coat with facing-colours borne on the collar, cuffs, lapels and turnbacks: Regt Prince Clement light green, Prince Albert

dark green, Prince John black and Polenz light blue. They had white breeches or (for service dress) grey overalls with red seam-stripe and often brown leather reinforcing. Officers wore similar dress with longer coat-tails, gold epaulettes, gold-laced belts, gold or silver shako-cords, white plume with black base and gold-laced 'Hessian' boots. Grey great-coats, often bearing the facing-colour on the collar; white leather equip-ment. Regt Prince Clement carried lances, with light green over red pennons (one source shows red over white); shabraques were red cloth, pointed-ended, with a border of the facing-colour, which had a zigzag inner edge and both edges piped yellow (gold for officers).

Trumpeters wore 'reversed' colours (the body of the coat in the regimental facing colour), except for Regt Prince John, whose trumpeters had chamois coats; all had red facings and yellow lace. In full dress trumpeters' coats had yellow-laced false sleeves, not worn on campaign. Shako was red with black leather reinforcing, yellow lace, white cords and red plume. On campaign the small pompom replaced the tall plume, and shako-cords were often removed on active service.

Though VII Corps' Saxon Chevau-legers suffered considerable loss, the survivors of Regt Prince John were captured en masse attempting to cover the crossing of the Berezina, while Prince Albert had scarcely 100 men left after Borodino, of whom only 14 officers and 12 other ranks survived the Retreat. See Plate 60, *Uniforms of the Napoleonic Wars.*

The Saxon Hussar Regiment wore a French-style uniform of similar shako with white cords and plume, light blue dolman with black facings and white braid, light blue pelisse with black fur and white braid, and white-laced light blue breeches.

The Saxon infantry adopted white French-style uniform and shako in 1810; grenadiers had red plumes and cords and the remainder white (the black-over-white plume normally restricted to N.C.O.s is found in some cases in illustrations probably representing privates). All Saxon troops wore white cockades. Officers had gold or silver shako-cords and lace, the shako's upper band being an inverted representation of the coronet-band of the Royal arms of Saxony. N.C.O. distinctions appear to have been confined to the lace band of regimental colour around the top of the shako. Though pointed cuffs are frequently illustrated, Opitz (among others) shows flat-topped cuffs. Officers wore longer coat-tails, gold epaulettes and gilt gorget. Facing-colours were borne on the collar, cuffs, lapels and piping of the shoulder straps and turnbacks (some sources show shoulder-straps of solid colour), and on the drummers' 'swallows' nest' wings; in 1810 these facings were as listed below.

In the 1813 list the title 'Prinz Clement' is changed to 'Steindel'; in the same year Prinz Friedrich August changed its facings to light blue. Equipment was of the French pattern; Opitz shows the cartridge-box bearing the FAR cypher as did the shako-plates, and drum-hoops of diagonal stripes of white and the facing colour.

The two Saxon light infantry regiments wore a similar dress, of

Regt	Facings	Buttons
König	scarlet	yellow
Niesemeuschel	scarlet	white
Prinz Anton	blue	white
Low	blue	yellow
Prinz Maximilian	yellow	yellow
Rechten	yellow	white
Prinz Friedrich August	green	yellow
Prinz Clement	green	white

dark green with black facings and red piping, brass buttons, grey breeches, brass shield-shaped shako-plates, green plume and cords. The two light infantry corps were raised in 1810 from the light companies of the line regiments, and are often confused with the Jägers (raised 1809), who wore similar uniform with hunting-horn shako-plate, black collar-patch, lighter green turnbacks, and grey breeches minus the red piping and 'darts' sometimes worn by the light infantry.

39. BERG: a) Officer, Infantry, full dress.
b) Pioneer, Infantry, full dress.
c) Musician, Infantry, campaign dress.

The veteran contingent supplied by the Grand Duchy of Cleve-Berg (mostly in IX Corps) was among the best of the Rhine Confederation forces, serving with distinction and suffering heavy losses. Even at Kovno the surviving Berg units still marched around their colours; of the seven infantry battalions only about 200 men survived the Retreat.

The four Berg regiments wore white French-style uniform with light blue collar, cuffs and lapels, all piped white; pocket-piping and turnbacks were light blue. The officer illustrated wears the 'old' coatee but the usual pattern was the short-tailed jacket with closed lapels. Both Suhr and Weiland show this uniform, Suhr showing pointed cuffs and Weiland flat-topped ones with flaps; perhaps both styles were used by different units. The French shako had three patterns of brass plate: two oval, one bearing the lion of Berg and one the initial J, and the third the diamond-shaped 'eagle' plate of the French army. Fusiliers had light blue shoulder-straps piped white, white shako-cords and pompom light blue or perhaps coloured by company as in the French army; chasseurs had white cords and green pompom, green epaulettes with green or red 'crescents' and green sword-knot with red tassel; grenadiers wore red or white shako-cords, red pompom, sword-knot and epaulettes. Their full dress bearskin cap had white or red cords, red rear patch bearing a white cross, red plume, but no plate; the red-edged-white Berg cockade was apparently not worn on the bearskin. Rank-markings were French, officers having gold epaulettes and bands on the shako, field officers wearing the bicorn with gold loop and national cockade. In service dress officers often wore a greyish-beige, single-breasted 'surtout' and breeches, with blue collar and cuffs and gold epaulettes; see Plate 67, *Uniforms of the Napoleonic Wars*.

The pioneer illustrated wears grenadier uniform and the unusual apron with coloured lace and bear-skin-fringe edging. The musician wears a 'service' uniform including loose trousers. Equipment was of French pattern, Knötel showing a grenadier (based on Suhr and Weiland) with a cartridge-box bearing a large brass bursting grenade badge.

40. BERG: a) Trooper, 2nd Chevau-Légers, campaign dress.
b) Trooper, Elite Company, 2nd Chevau-Légers.

The Berg cavalry regiment was raised in May 1807 by Murat (then Grand Duke of Berg) as the Chevau-Légers de Berg, reconstituted in 1808 as the Chasseurs à Cheval de Berg, changing in December 1809 to the Lanciers de

Berg. In 1812 (when the original unit was serving in Spain) a second regiment of Chevau-Légers-Lanciers was raised, ultimately titled the 2nd Chevau-Légers de Berg, the first three squadrons of which (sometimes titled '1st Lancers') served in the Grande Armée, its 180 survivors being compelled to surrender at Borisov; only two companies serving with Marshal Victor escaped, joining the 4th Squadron until wiped out in an ambush in 1813.

The élite company trooper illustrated is partly taken from Knötel, who shows Chasseur à Cheval uniform in use as late as 1812; however, it is likely that the dress worn in Russia was a combination of the later lancer style (with pointed cuffs and pink seam-piping), with busby with 'amaranth' bag retained until 1813 by the élites. The later style repeated the colouring introduced in 1808, dark green with 'amaranth' facings; the lapels were 'amaranth' in full dress but could be buttoned over to show as dark green with 'amaranth' piping in service dress. Red epaulettes and plume were worn by élites. Apart from the squadrons in Spain (who wore green surtouts and 'amaranth' shakos) the lancer uniform included 'amaranth'-topped czapka with white lace and brass plate, and white cords and plume in full dress, with waterproof cover on campaign. The trooper in campaign dress wears a rolled cloak and service overalls (alternatively dark grey with 'amaranth' stripe); full dress wear was either dark green breeches and boots, or similar overalls with buttons on the outer seam.

Lance-pennons were 'amaranth' over white.

Though it seems unlikely that full dress was ever extensively worn, Knötel shows its use with pointed-ended 'amaranth' shabraque; other sources show plainer horse-furniture of a white sheepskin with 'amaranth' wolf-tooth edging, and white-laced 'amaranth' valise. A trumpeter is shown wearing a green-topped czapka with brass plate, white lace and cords and yellow ball-tuft, and 'Imperial Livery' (green jacket with mixed yellow and green lace) with 'amaranth' facings and lapels, white epaulettes, grey overalls with 'amaranth' stripe, and black sheepskin shabraque with 'amaranth' wolf-tooth edging.

41. BADEN: a) Trooper, Hussars. b) Officer, Hussars, with standard.

The Baden contingent (about 9,000 men) has often been regarded as the best German formation in the 'Grande Armée'. The single cavalry regiment won great fame when ordered to protect the rear of the army at the Berezina. With the Hessian Chevaulegers (Plate 42) the Baden Hussars made the famous 'Charge of Death' from which only fifty men of each regiment returned. Commanded by Col. von Laroche (Col. von Cancrin had been killed two weeks before), the Hussars drove in a square of the 34th Russian Jägers but were destroyed by a reinforcement of Russian cuirassiers.

The Baden Hussars wore French-style uniform: shako with yellow cords (gold cords and lace for officers), dark green dolman with red facings and yellow braid, dark green pelisse with black or dark brown fur and yellow braid, red breeches with yellow lace, Hessian boots, and dark green sabretache with yellow border and central lace device consisting of a crown over CF (cypher of the Grand Duke of Baden). On campaign waterproof shako-covers, the pelisse worn as a jacket, rolled cloak over one shoulder, plain black sabretache, and either grey or dark green overalls with red stripe were worn. Officers wore the frock-coat illustrated, similar to the Prussian 'litewka'. The red sash with yellow barrels was not worn with the coat and was obscured when the pelisse was worn as a jacket. White leather equipment was worn, officers having red pouch-belts with gold lace edging or central stripe, and black sword-belts.

Features shown by various sources include green shako-plumes (full dress), white-over-red (field officer), black, or black with red tip and base (warrant officer), and white or yellow shako-pompoms worn on service with or without the shako-cover. N.C.O.s wore yellow lace around the top of the shako, one illustration showing their red breeches with 'Austrian knot' decoration only slightly less elaborate than the officers'; a field officer is shown in French chasseur à cheval dress, green coatee with red facings and piping to the green lapels, cut open to expose a gold-braided red waistcoat, red-striped grey trousers, black bicorn hat with green-over-red plume and plain green cloth shabraque with red lace edging (after Hourtoulle). Other

details shown with field officers' hussar costume are white pelisse-fur and green Hessian boots with gold lace.

Trumpeters wore red shako with yellow lace upper band and green plume, red dolman with green facings and yellow braid, red pelisse with brown fur and yellow braid, and red overalls; another source shows a similar uniform but with black plume and leather bands on the shako, and green overalls with red stripe. Officers' shabraques had gold lace and crowned CF in the rear corners, and black sheepskin, while red 'wolf-tooth' edging is shown on the sheepskins of the rank and file in one illustration. Trumpeters had shabraques like the troopers but with black sheepskins edged red.

The regimental standard was white with ornate gold-embroidered ornaments in the corners and the Arms of Baden in the centre, supported by two golden griffins on gold ornamental scroll, with ermine mantle and golden crown above.

42. HESSE-DARMSTADT:
a) Trumpeter, Chevaulegers.
FRANCE: b) Trooper, Portuguese Legion Cavalry.
c) Officer, Portuguese Legion Cavalry.

Prior to 1812 the cavalry of the Portuguese Legion wore a fur-crested helmet, lapelled jacket and light blue breeches, but changed to brown surtout with red facings and piping, silver epaulettes for officers and red for other ranks (perhaps restricted to the élite company, an illustration of the earlier uniform showing brown shoulder-straps piped red which may have continued on the new dress), and either grey or brown overalls with one or two red stripes, or brown breeches with either red stripe or white stripe and 'darts' on the thighs. French-style shako with pompom (red or green, or coloured by company?), tricolor cockade and plate bearing an eagle were worn, though some (perhaps élites) possessed a plain black fur busby, minus decorations. A picture in Ribeiro's work on the Legion shows an officer with busby bearing red pompom, and silver-laced pouch-belt (both details also shown in a German engraving); and Faber du Faur shows an officer wearing a large cloak and shako in a waterproof cover; according to a directive of 12 June 1812 the great-coat/cloak was to be of the same colour as the jacket. Officers had pointed-ended, chasseur à cheval style shabraques of red with wide silver lace edging; other ranks had cream sheepskins with red 'wolf-tooth' edging.

The small Hesse-Darmstadt contingent (5,000 men) was excellent in quality, the Chevaulegers participating in the 'Charge of Death' at Studianka (see Plate 41); only 42 men and 21 horses of this fine regiment returned home. They wore a Bavarian-style black leather helmet with black crest and a large front-plate (which design is shown differently by contemporary sources) of black leather with brass edging,

bearing a brass crown over the L cypher of Grand Duke Ludwig X. For all except trumpeters the plume was black over red, rising from red-and-white Hessian cockade. The troopers' uniform was like that illustrated, minus the lace and with white loops on the lapels; breeches either white or green (green overalls with red stripe and black leather reinforcing in service dress); black leather equipment. Officers had silver lace and helmet-fittings and silver-laced belts. Dark green pointed-ended shabraques with black lace edging piped white were seen, bearing crowned cypher in white in the rear corners (silver lace for officers). See Plate 49, *Uniforms of the Napoleonic Wars*.

The Hesse-Darmstadt infantry wore French-style uniform, including the shako with white metal plates (of the same shapes as the French) bearing the Hessian lion; the Leib-Garde had white metal chinscales and the others black chinstraps edged with the facing colour. Above the national cockade was a pompom, yellow, black, blue or red for the 1st to 4th Companies respectively, N.C.O.s having red pompom with white horizontal ring and tuft; the Leib-Garde had black feather plumes in full dress, the officers' with red base and N.C.O.s' with red tip. The jacket was like the French 1812 pattern, dark blue with facings borne on collar, lapels, cuffs and piping to the cuff-flaps, turnbacks and shoulder-straps; turnback-badges were grenades and hunting-horns of the facing colour for grenadiers and voltigeurs respectively. Facing-colours were: Leib-Garde, red; Leib-Regiment, light blue; and

Leib-Fusiliers, scarlet. The fourth unit, Garde-Fusiliers, was a provisional light infantry corps formed on 1 March 1812 from the Leib-Garde and Leib-Fusiliers. On active service, loose blue or white trousers and gaiters were worn for winter and summer respectively; shakos were often covered, and lapels buttoned over to conceal the facings (though officers of the Leib-Garde were ordered to wear the longer-tailed dress coat with laced lapels buttoned back for the campaign); officers had silver lace, epaulettes and sash, light blue trousers and knee-boots, and often wore the single-breasted surtout in regimental colouring.

Interesting variations are recorded by Capt. Franz Roeder of the Leib-Garde; on 25 August, for example (St. Louis' Day, patron saint of the Grand Duke) the regiment wore full dress, though even before the Retreat the regimental tailors had to manufacture uniforms from cloth taken from a Polish unit, 'for my soldiers' coats are falling to pieces on their backs'. Roeder himself soon lost the appearance of an officer, wearing a fur cap made by his sergeant-major and a bloodstained fur coat with a hole in it, marking the course of a roundshot which had killed its previous owner, a French voltigeur officer. In December Roeder's wardrobe consisted of various civilian items, a blue Russian frock-coat, two French 'patent hats' (forage caps), English top-boots, a blue fur-lined cap, one of his original uniform coats, blue trousers, grey gaiters, a fox-fur coat, and a French Imperial Guard sword!

43. AUSTRIA: a) Trooper, 4th Hussars, service dress.
b) Sutleress, 1st Hussars, service dress.

The Austrian hussar shako had yellow rosette and black-and-yellow national pompom, with cords (when worn) looped up on campaign in Russian style; plumes not worn on campaign. The sprig of leaves worn behind the pompom was a national distinction. The dolman, collar, cuffs and pelisse were of the same colour, the pelisse often worn as a jacket on service, all but obscuring the black-barrelled yellow sash. Button-colour varied but braid was always mixed yellow-and-black (gold braid and shako-lace for officers). Grey overalls were used on campaign but contemporary prints suggest that the full dress breeches (with 'Austrian knot' decoration on the thighs) were worn on occasion. Sabretaches were of uniform pattern, red with yellow and black lace and yellow crowned FL cypher. The official colouring of the 4th (Hessen-Homburg) Hussars illustrated was – in the terminology of the Austrian Army – 'pale blue' shako, 'parrot-green' jacket and pelisse, 'light red' breeches and white metal buttons.

The Sutleress is taken from a contemporary print possibly showing the semi-official uniform of the 1st (Kaiser Franz) Regt, which wore black shako, dark blue jacket, pelisse and breeches, and brass buttons. Many regiments had attendant lady sutleresses whose costume was frequently coloured like that of their regiment.

Shabraques were red, pointed-ended, with edging of yellow and black lace and bearing the same device as the sabretache in the rear corners. Valises were red, and sheepskin saddle-covers (often black) were also used. Another of the Grande Armée's Austrian Hussar regiments, the 6th (Blankenstein), wore a most striking dress: black shako, 'cornflower blue' jacket, pelisse and breeches, and brass buttons.

44. AUSTRIA: a) Grenadier officer, 30th Regt.
b) Fusilier officer, 48th Regt, campaign dress.

The traditional white Austrian uniform bore the facing-colour on the cuffs, collar, turnbacks and shoulder-straps; a single fringed lace loop decorated the pointed cuffs of Hungarian regiments. White breeches and black knee-length gaiters indicated 'German' regiments, Hungarians having tight sky-blue breeches with mixed yellow-and-black braid and ankle-boots; all officers wore black boots, with or without metallic lace edging.

The grenadier wears the distinctive fur cap, which from its high front peak and low rear section was nicknamed 'fauteuil' (armchair) by the French; the colouring of the rear patch seems to have varied, either yellow or the facing colour, with white wavy lace decoration. Officers' coatees had longer tails than those of the other ranks, from 1811 officially with white turnbacks, though some sources show the coloured style persisting: see Plate 5, *World Uniforms and Battles 1815–50*. Grenadier officers frequently adopted pistols carried in holsters on shoulder-belts and curved sabres as carried by Hungarian regiments. Fusiliers wore the shako with metallic lace and pompom for officers, yellow rosette and black-and-yellow pompom for privates and a yellow lace band around the top for N.C.O.s. The Hungarian wears the dark grey 'caputrock' frock-coat, often used on campaign; other ranks' greatcoats were of a browner shade. His sash is tied in a bow to prevent the hanging tails from entangling with the sabre. Facing-colours for some of the regiments in the Austrian Reserve Corps were:

Regt		Nationality	Facings	Buttons
9	(Czartoryski)	Galician	apple-green	yellow
19	(Alvinzy)	Hungarian	sky-blue	white
30	(Prinz de Ligne)	Walloon	light blue-grey	yellow
34	(Daidovitz)	Hungarian	madder-red	white
41	(Sattulinski)	Galician	sulphur-yellow	white
48	(Simbschen)	Hungarian	steel-green	yellow

The attached 'Grenz' or frontier infantry wore infantry shako, short-tailed brown jacket with coloured collar, turnbacks and pointed cuffs (crab-red with white buttons for the 'Sankt Georger' (St. George) regiment for example), Hungarian breeches and cuff-lace. See also Plates 32 and 39, *Uniforms of the Napoleonic Wars*.

45. KINGDOM OF ITALY:
a) Grenadier, 2nd Line, full dress.
PRUSSIA: b) Fusilier, 3rd (2nd East Prussian) Regt, full dress.

The Italian infantry battalion consisted of four fusilier, one grenadier and one voltigeur company; the French-style uniform comprised a long-tailed white coatee (the 1812 French pattern adopted in only limited quantities in 1813) with coloured facings. The French-style shako's diamond-shaped plate bore the Iron Crown of Lombardy over the regimental number; the later 'eagle' plate was also worn, and the design of the red, white and green Italian 'tricolor' cockade sometimes alternated to distinguish between battalions. The shako had a black cover for active service. Fusiliers had white shoulder-straps piped as the lapels; grenadiers wore black bear-skin with brass plate, red rear patch bearing a white cross, red epaulettes, sword-knot, plume (also worn on the shako) and cords (silver for officers); voltigeurs had green 'carrot'-shaped shako-pompom, green epaulettes and

green sword-knot with white tassel. Turnback and cartridge-box badges were of the grenade and hunting-horn where appropriate. Officers had French rank-markings and equipment and silver lace.

Of the regiments in the 'Grande Armée', the 2nd had white collar and cuffs, green cuff-flaps, red lapels, turnbacks and piping, and the 3rd green lapels, cuffs, turnbacks and piping and red collar and cuff-flaps (Leinhart & Humbert show the 2nd with red cuff-flaps and white turn-backs and red piping on all but the lapels and cuff-flaps, and the 3rd with all items red piped white save for red piping on the shoulder-straps); buttons brass for both. The 1st and 3rd Light Infantry had infantry shakos with plates bearing the regimental number inside a hunting-horn, red cords for carabiniers, green for voltigeurs and white for chasseurs, dark green French light infantry coatees with collar, cuff-flaps and piping to the pockets, lapels, cuffs and turnbacks of yellow for the 1st and orange for the 3rd; both wore dark green breeches, the 1st yellow waist-coats and the 3rd dark green; carabiniers at times wore a bearskin cap (without plate) and voltigeurs a green plume in full dress. Regimental variations are recorded.

The Prussian 'Combined Infantry' units comprised battalions taken from line regiments. The 1808 shako had white lace band and black-and-white pompom, with a lace rosette and loop (fusiliers), the FWR royal cypher (musketeers) or brass eagle (grena-diers); the shako had a black water-proof cover on campaign, officers' caps having gold lace band, gilt ornaments and gilt chains hung around. The 'kollet' coatee was dark blue with red turnbacks and brass buttons, longer-tailed for officers who had cloth epaulettes with silver lace edging and metal 'crescents' and fusilier's straight-bladed 'faschinen-messer' sword. The East Prussian Jäger battalion had a similar dress of dark green with scarlet collar and cuffs, lace shako-rosette, grey breeches black equipment and green sword-knot. Musket-slings were red-brown

Regt		Collar and Cuffs	Shoulder-straps
1st	(1st East Prussian)	brick red	white
2nd	(1st Pommeranian)	white	white
3rd	(2nd East Prussian)	brick red	scarlet
4th	(3rd East Prussian)	brick red	yellow
5th	(4th East Prussian)	brick red	light blue
6th	(1st West Prussian)	crimson	white
7th	(2nd West Prussian)	crimson	scarlet
9th	(Leib-Regiment)	scarlet	white
10th	(Colberg)	white	scarlet
11th	(1st Silesian)	lemon yellow	white
12th	(2nd Silesian)	lemon yellow	scarlet

silver-and-black waist-sash. The collar and cuffs indicated the regiment's region of origin and the shoulder-straps the seniority (i.e. 1st East Prussian, etc.). Elements of the following served with the 'Grande Armée':

Breeches were white or grey (summer and winter) with black gaiters (grey overalls for officers). Equipment consisted of hide knapsack, white belts (black for fusiliers) and black cartridge-box (worn at the front by fusiliers who wore only one shoulder-belt), bearing an oval brass plate with the Prussian eagle for all except fusiliers, those of the Leib-Regiment having a five-pointed star. Greatcoats were grey; the infantry sabre had a knot coloured by company, or a distinctive black-and-white 'honour knot' reserved for veterans of the 1806 campaign, illustrated here on the for all. See also Plate 69, *Uniforms of Waterloo*, and Plate 69, *Uniforms of the Napoleonic Wars*.

46. a) BERG: Private, Foot Artillery.
   b) BAVARIA: Private, Foot Artillery.
   c) FRANCE: Drummer, Line Foot Artillery.

The French Foot Artillery wore dark blue with red facings and dark blue breeches, though the drummer illustrated (from the *Collections Alsaciennes*) wears 'reversed colours' with large wings. The usual styles were adopted on campaign; Col. Griois, commanding the artillery of III Cavalry Corps, described his uniform during the Retreat: a flannel waist-coat under a red cashmere waiscoat, over which a linen dress-coat, then a frock-coat, with linen trousers buttoned on the sides and tight knee-boots; over all a fur-coat (until it was stolen at the Berezina), after which a bearskin pelt over the shoulders, plus strips of bearskin serving as a stole around the neck, a muff (he had no gloves) and a lining to his stirrups to keep his feet warm; his 'battered hat' was worn over a strip of fur which covered his chin and the bottom part of his face and tied behind the head. Griois noted that thus attired he was one of very few 'whose costume still preserved some vestiges of uniform'.

The Berg Foot Artillery uniform (after Knötel) was similar to the French, excepting the absence of shako-plate and the red-and-white cockade. Other sources show a shield-shaped plate bearing the letter N, and Peter Schulten (who painted troops he saw passing through Wuppertal) shows a dark blue uniform with black collar, cuffs, lapels, turnbacks and shoulder-straps, all piped red. On campaign dark blue overalls with red stripe were worn. The Berg contingent lost all their guns in Russia.

The Bavarian Foot Artillery wore a uniform like the infantry, with red-plumed leather helmet, and dark blue uniform with black facings, brass shoulder-scales, and red piping. Officers had gold lace, but discontinued the sash in April 1812, officers of light batteries receiving a black leather cartridge-box and shoulder-belt in its place. The Artillery Train wore similar dress but of grey with blue facings, and light grey overalls with blue stripe.

See also Plates 68 and 75, *Uniforms of the Napoleonic Wars*, and Plates 52 and 60, *Uniforms of Waterloo*.

47. FRANCE: a) 'Flanquer', Imperial Guard.
b) Driver, Artillery Train, Imperial Guard.
c) 'Infirmier', Service du Santé (Medical Corps).

A corps of Guard 'Flanquers' was raised in September 1811, termed 'Flanquer-Grenadiers' when the 'Flanquer-Chasseurs' were formed in March 1813. The uniform illustrated comes from a Martinet print showing full dress; another version shows a plume with a thinner lower section and a smaller, flatter upper part. The red turnbacks probably bore white eagle badges.

Illustrated is a common method of evacuating wounded by seating them on a musket; both Adam and Bayer show its use in 1812–13 sketches. The medical orderlies wore red-brown infantry uniforms with red facings and white piping, and carried sabres and muskets. The 'Infirmier' illustrated carries his medical equipment in a satchel over one shoulder; another pattern consisted of a waistbelt worn under the coatee with a long, narrow satchel at the front. Not until surgeon Percy organised his 'infirmiers-brancardiers' (stretcher-bearers) in about 1813 were the orderlies given collapsible stretchers which fitted on to the shafts of pikes they carried.

Medical services were woefully inefficient, despite the efforts of a few humanitarian officers like Baron

Larrey, whom Napoleon called 'the most virtuous man I knew'. Larrey devised a light, two-wheeled ambulance to evacuate casualties as quickly as possible and endeavoured to bring about wholesale improvement in the standards of medical care; one of the 'unsung heroes' of the Napoleonic Wars he deserves to be remembered more than the perpetrators of the bloodshed he tried to assuage. He apparently wore two uniforms during the campaign: one, from February to April, was that of the Surgeon-in-Chief of the Imperial Guard, consisting of black bicorn with 'tricolor' cockade, gold loop and tassels, blue lapelled 'habit' closed to the waist with crimson collar, pointed cuffs, turnbacks and lapel-piping with gold-edged collar and cuffs and two gold loops on the collar, gold crowned N on the turnbacks, gold aiguillette on the right shoulder, white breeches and gold-laced 'Hessian' boots; the other from April to December as Surgeon-in-Chief of the 'Grande Armée', the same but with single-breasted 'surtout', crimson collar and flat-topped cuffs with double row of gold leaf-embroidery, crimson turnbacks and the aiguillette as before.

The Imperial Guard Artillery Train wore 'steel-grey' uniforms with dark blue facings, the version shown apparently adopted in 1812, before which a similarly-coloured 'habit' with pointed cuffs and trefoil epaulettes had been worn, shown by Martinet in full dress with 'steel-grey' breeches with red stripe and Austrian knot on the thighs, red-laced 'Hessian' boots, shako with red lace bands, plume and cords, and 'steel-grey', red-braided waistcoat.

The gaiters illustrated are of an uncommon pattern, cut low over the heel. With 'regulation dress' depending upon the interpretation of often unclear descriptions by local manufacturers, many styles would inevitably result. The more usual pattern, cut higher at the rear, is shown in other plates.

48. FRANCE: a) Marshal Ney.
b) Infantryman,
campaign dress.

The career of Marshal Michel Ney (1769–1815) can be summarised by his best-known sobriquet: 'The Bravest of the Brave'. His unfailing loyalty and famed heroism passed into legend during the Retreat when, commanding the rearguard of the wrecked 'Grande Armée', he held the ragged band together by force of personality, fighting with them, musket in hand, against overwhelming odds. Attempting to hold Kovno and its bridge with only 1,000 men against Platov's cossacks, Ney was compelled to burn the bridge and withdraw, the last Frenchman to leave Russian soil. Like Murat, Ney faced death a thousand times on the battlefield only to die by firing-squad.

Ney is illustrated wearing his Marshal's hat minus its feathers, and a fur-lined overcoat; this dress is shown by Faber du Faur and Grenadier Pils, though one portrait (painted after the campaign) shows gold braid on the greatcoat-breast. Ney carries a cavalry sabre and a musket picked off the road. Count Dumas saw him at the end, 'wearing a brown coat . . . he had a long beard. His face was black and seemed to be burnt. His eyes were red and glistening. "What! Don't you recognise me? I am the rearguard of the Grande Armée, Marshal Ney. I fired the last shot on the bridge at Kovno . . .".'

The infantry private is principally taken from an Adam picture showing a sentry 'before Moscow', with shako-cover let down to form a type of balaklava helmet. The mittens, gloves and fur boots are privately-acquired. In addition to such improvisations members of the 'Grande Armée' adopted Russian peasant footwear, described by a contemporary observer in the 'Royal Military Chronicle' of 1812: 'Besides one or two pairs of worsted stockings, they add wrappers of coarse flannel, or cloth, several feet in length, and over these, frequently draw a pair of boots, so large as to receive the whole bulk.'

49. FRANCE: a) Trooper, 23rd Chasseurs à Cheval.
   b) 'Premier Porte-Aigle', 7th Light Infantry.
   c) Cuirassier.

During the Retreat every imaginable item was used in an attempt to combat the cold; frequently two or more greatcoats were worn, stuffed with whatever scraps could be found or stripped from the half-buried corpses in the snow along the route.

The 23rd Chasseurs à Cheval was commanded by Colonel A.-M. Marbot, who several days east of Vilna realised that the regiment would become divided as horses died from cold and exhaustion. He therefore dismounted the unit and used the surviving horses to pull small, two-man sledges which could be found in every Russian peasant dwelling. With the 24th Chasseurs they formed a sledge-transported brigade which could defend itself admirably, Marbot ordering every man to take two muskets and a cartridge-box from those abandoned on the road, to enable them to beat off attacks with 'the liveliest musketry'. At night the sledges formed a square like a 'Wild West' waggon-train, making a mobile fort in which Marshal Ney and General Maison (commanding II Corps after Oudinot's wound) frequently took shelter. The chasseur illustrated wears busby minus ornaments, fur-bound footwear and a shabraque (or two strapped together) for additional warmth, its 'wolf-tooth' edging of the 'dark orange' facing-colour. The cartridge-box is carried in the most accessible position.

The 7th Light Infantry officer wears a fur pelt around his shoulders and a fur-lined forage-cap, of which numerous varieties existed, all privately-made; the version illustrated is taken from Faber du Faur. The 'Eagle' is carried minus the flag (a common practice on campaign); that of the 7th had one wing carried away by a Russian ball at Eylau. Of the 7th's 4,163 men who had embarked on the campaign, less than 700 remained around their 'Eagle' in December. Lieut. Dufour, 'Premier-Porte-Aigle' from September 1810, was killed on 16 December. See black-and-white Plate G.

The cuirassier is taken from a picture by J. A. Klein, and wears a piece of sacking over his head and a length of carpet as a rudimentary cloak.

50. RUSSIA: a) Trooper, Starodub Cuirassiers, service dress.
        b) Officer, Chevalier-Gardes, full dress.
        c) General Kutuzov.

The Russian staff uniform introduced in 1808 consisted of double-breasted dark green coatee with red turnbacks (single-breasted for cavalry generals), with red collar and cuffs heavily embroidered in gold palm and laurel design, repeated on the pocket-flaps. Gold epaulettes, aiguillette on the right shoulder, and the usual silver sash with interwoven orange and black strands were worn. With this full dress was worn a black bicorn with white over black-and-orange feathers, and white breeches with black Hessian or knee-boots. On campaign an unlaced coatee and grey overalls were common, but variations existed. The illustration of Kutuzov is based principally on a portrait by George Dawe who shows a large fur-lined coat; Kutuzov apparently favoured a plain service dress, with either dress coatee minus decorations, as shown by some (non-contemporary) Russian artists, or a greatcoat and forage-cap. At Borodino he was described wearing a 'round white forage-cap and dark green overcoat without epaulettes'.

The heavy cavalry comprised cuirassiers and dragoons, with the Chevalier-Gardes, originally the Czar's bodyguard raised by Peter the Great, included in the cuirassier arm. The uniform illustrated conforms to the 1812 regulations, the old 'round' helmet-crest replaced by the horsehair 'brush' variety, and the collar lower and closed (as in all Russian uniforms after the 1812 regulations). The black leather helmet was similar for all regiments, bearing the Imperial eagle (silver star for the Chevalier-Gardes and the Order of St. George for the Military Order Regt). The white coatee bore facing-colours on the collar, cuffs and shoulder-straps: Chevalier-Gardes and Horse Guard red, Life Guard and Starodub light blue, Czarina's violet, Ekaterinoslav orange, Pskoff dark red, Glukhov blue, Astrachan yellow, Military Order black, Little Russia dark green, and Novgorod light red. White lace was worn by the Life Guard, Czarina's, Ekaterinoslav, Astrachan and Novgorod, and yellow for the remainder (silver or gold for officers), and loops of 'Guard' lace – a straight bar with a 'dart' at the ends – for the Chevalier-Gardes, Horse Guard and Life Guard. The white full dress breeches and long boots were replaced on campaign by grey-brown overalls for the rank and file, and grey overalls (sometimes with a stripe of the facing colour) for officers, with or without leather reinforcing.

Officers wore metallic lace epaulettes; the rank and file had white leather equipment. All wore the cuirass, the German pattern consisting only of a front-plate, but probably a version with backplate was worn by some cuirassiers in 1812. The backless version was certainly used, the French Col. Combe noting how at Borodino the French were able 'to do great execution by thrusting at them as they fled'. The cuirasses were effective from the front, however; when the French 9th Chevau-Légers-Lanciers mistakenly ran headlong into a Russian cuirassier corps in gathering gloom, they found their lances unable to penetrate the breast-plates and fell back in disorder. The cuirasses were black-enamelled iron with brass fittings (gilt for officers) for all except the Czarina's Regt (white metal cuirasses) and the Pskoff (white metal for rank and file, gilt for officers). Shabraques were square-ended, red, and edged with either white or yellow lace (yellow with blue or black line for the Chevaliers-Gardes, yellow with red line for Horse Guard); officers' shabraques had metallic lace edging (silver with white line for Life Guard). The rear corners of the shabraque bore the Imperial cypher or regimental badge, holster-caps being the same design as the shabraque, with the same badge. The Chevalier-Gardes squadrons were mounted on horses of distinctive colours: 1st and 5th bays, 2nd chestnuts, 3rd greys and 4th blacks. See also black-and-white Plate C.

51. RUSSIA: a) N.C.O., Kinburn Dragoons.
b) Trooper, Moscow Dragoons.

Russian dragoons wore a helmet like the cuirassiers, the brass plate bearing the Imperial eagle. The double-breasted dark green jacket had collar, cuffs and shoulder-straps of the regimental facing colour, and red turnbacks; grey overalls were worn by all ranks. Officers had silver epaulettes, buttons and sash, and N.C.O.s silver lace edging to the collar and cuffs. Shabraques were round-ended with lace edging and Imperial cypher in the rear corners in the facing colour, the cypher in silver for officers. White belts bore brass fittings, the black leather pouch bearing circular brass plate embossed with the Imperial eagle. Sword-scabbards were of brown leather.

Of the thirty-six Russian line dragoon regiments, half were converted on 10 November 1812 to form two regiments of cuirassiers, one of hussars, seven of lancers and eight of mounted rifles. Few of these can have received their new uniform before the beginning of 1813, excepting perhaps men at regimental depots.

The dragoon facing-colours (after Knötel) were as follows, regiments marked * having green collars with piping of the facing colour, the letters w or y indicating white or yellow metal buttons: Riga, red, y; Jamburg *, green, w; Kasan, carmine, y; Njeschin *, light blue, y; Pskoff, orange, y; Moscow, pink, w; Kargopol, orange, w; Ingermanland, black, w; Kurland, light blue, y; Orenburg, black, y; Sibirien, white, w; Irkutsk, white, y; Kharkov, dark yellow, y; Chernigov, blue, w; Kiev, carmine, w; New Russia, light blue, w; Starodub, red, w; Twer, blue, y; Schitomir, red, w; Arsamass *, light blue, w; St. Petersburg, pink, y;

Livland, red, Y; Sjewersk, dark yellow, W; Kinburn, yellow, W; Smolensk, yellow, Y; Perejeslaw *, carmine, W; Tiraspol *, red, Y; Dorpat *, yellow, W; Wladimir *, white, Y; Taganrok *, pink, Y; Serpuchow *, yellow, Y; Nischegorod *, white, W; Narwa *, pink, W; Borissoglebsk *, carmine, Y; Finland, white, Y; Mitau, white, W. In addition, Regts Schitomir and Livland had white collar-piping, and Regts Finland and Mitau red. The Lifeguard Dragoons wore similar uniform, but with yellow 'Guard' pattern lace (gold for officers) on their red collars and cuffs.

52. RUSSIA: a) Trooper, Isum Hussars.
b) Trooper, Elisavetgrad Hussars.
c) Trooper, Litovski Lancers.

The hussar uniform illustrated is that worn prior to the 1812 regulations, the new uniform not being issued to all units in time for the campaign. The older uniform – pelisse, dolman and barrelled sash – was worn with 'stovepipe' shako, which had lace decorations (metallic for officers) and cords, these usually wrapped once or twice around the cap and allowed to hang down, but wrapped a third time on campaign to shorten the length, and sometimes looped over the pompom. Officers had chains suspended around the cap and hooked on to metal Imperial eagle badges on the sides. Grey overalls were worn on campaign, but the Isum Hussar illustrated wears the dark blue sketched by the anonymous artist of the Elberfeld Manuscript, who shows the dolman worn only, apparently not simply a concession to warm weather as the picture is dated 2 February 1814. The shako in the Elberfeld picture has red cords and plume, and the man carries a lance with red-over-blue pennon. The Elisavetgrad Hussar from the same source also wears the 'old' cap, the pelisse worn as a jacket, and a black-faced sabretache. See text to Plate 53 for regulation Hussar colouring.

The six Russian Lancer regiments (not including the dragoons converted at the end of the year) wore high-crowned czapkas, the tops of black leather and the sides cloth (the top as well for officers), with white or yellow lace and cockades (Litovski Regt raspberry-red cockades). White plumes, with black-and-orange tip for N.C.O.s, who had scarlet cockades with lace cross-strips of mixed white-and-orange; white or yellow cords (silver for officers), the Guard Lancers having the large yellow metal Guard eagle-plate on the front of the cap. Dark blue jacket with collar, lapels, cuffs and piping on the rear seams and turnbacks in the facing colour; the Guard wore two 'Guard' loops on the collar (N.C.O.s one) and one on the cuff, of yellow with red stripe (gold for officers). Dark blue trousers were worn with two stripes and piping between of the facing colour; blue girdle with two facing-coloured stripes (silver sashes for officers); white leather equipment (red leather waist-belts for the Guard). Pouch-belt gold-laced for guard officers and metallic-laced white leather for the line. Epaulettes of the button-colour. Greyish-buff greatcoats for all except officers, who had silver-grey greatcoats with facing-coloured collarpatch, seam-piping and epaulettes. Dark blue rounded-ended shabraques with lace edging, piping and Imperial cypher in the rear corners, of the facing colour (mixed red-and-yellow for the Guard, gold for Guard officers). Trumpeters had laced jackets (as in Plate 62), the lace white (white with red stripe for the Guard). Lances were carried by the front rank of each regiment, with pennons of two colours, with two narrow central lines of alternately-coloured material. Regimental details were:

GUARD: facings red, buttons yellow, pennon white over red.
VOLYNSKI: facings, raspberry-red; blue czapka-tops, white buttons, pennon red over white.
LITOVSKI: facings and cap-cords raspberry-red, buttons and czapkatops white, pennon white over dark blue.
POLISH: facings raspberry-red, white buttons, dark blue czapka-tops, pennon blue over raspberry-red.
TATARSKI: facings and czapka-tops raspberry-red, white buttons, pennon blue over raspberry-red.
TCHOUGAIEOSKI: facings and czapka-tops raspberry-red, white buttons, pennon red over blue.

The Elberfeld Manuscript shows a trooper of the Polish Regt, dated 12 February 1814, wearing plumeless czapka, white lace edging around the collar, white fringed epaulettes, tight grey overalls with brass buttons on the outer seam, black pouch and belt and blue pennon.

53. RUSSIA: a) Trooper, Pavlograd Hussars. b) 'Flanker', Elisavetgrad Hussars.

Both hussars wear the 1812 regulation uniform, including the lower, closed collar and the individually-Russian 'kiwer' shako, a scuttle-shaped cap with concave top, probably designed by Czar Alexander himself. The shako-cords were usually worn even on campaign, looped over the pompom so as not to impede movement. The full dress plume was never worn on campaign. The hussars (after Knötel) wear the dolman without pelisse and leather-reinforced service overalls; note the leather elbow- and heart-shaped knee-patches. The sabretache was similar for all regiments, but in regimental colouring. The front rank of hussar regiments was armed with lances, and sixteen men of each squadron were equipped with carbines to act as 'flankers'. The 1801 pattern sabre was short and heavy-bladed by European standards, but many contemporary pictures show Russian troops (particularly cavalry) carrying captured weapons. Horse-furniture was a standard design for all regiments.

A number of variations are shown by different sources, for example the lace and braid of the Elisavetgrad; Knötel shows this yellow, though the regulations specified red braid. Red is shown by the Elberfeld Manuscript (see Plate 52), and additional information is given by 'Capt. Fritz', an anonymous German officer who had served under Wellington in the Peninsular War before transferring to Russian service in the Elisavetgrad Hussars. He noted that the summer of Alexandrinsk black/scarlet; Sumski and Bieloserk scarlet/white; Elisavetgrad dark green/yellow; Grodno and Lubenski dark blue/sky blue; Isum dark blue/white; Mariupol dark blue/yellow, and dark green/scarlet for the remainder. The Life Guard Hussars wore dark blue dolman with scarlet facings and pelisse, yellow lace, white

Regt	Pelisse	Dolman	Collar/cuffs	Lace	Buttons
Isum	blue	red	blue	white	white
Grodno	blue	blue	light blue	white	white
Lubenski	blue	blue	yellow	white	white
Mariupol	blue	blue	yellow	yellow	yellow
Bieloserk	brown	blue	red	white	white
Akhtyrka	red	brown	yellow	yellow	yellow
Alexandrinsk	black	black	red	white	white
Pavlograd	light blue	green	light blue	red	yellow
Elisavetgrad	grey	grey	grey	red	yellow
Sumski	grey	grey	red	white	white
Olwiopol	green	green	red	white	white

1812 was so dry and hot that the dust rose in choking clouds at the slightest movement, so that 'the dust lay so thick on my dark grey dolman, which was faced [i.e. braided] with red, that it was no longer possible to make out the slightest trace of this colour . . .'.

Uniform-colours of the line hussars (after Knötel) were as listed above. Other sources show different details, for example the Pavlograd with yellow lace. Knötel gives white pelisse-fur for all except the Bieloserk and Elisavetgrad (black), but other sources indicate that officers wore white and other ranks black. Trousers black for the Alexandrinsk, Elisavetgrad and Pavlograd dark green, Olwiopol scarlet, and dark blue for the remainder. Sabretaches were: Achtirsk brown with yellow lace; trousers and pelisse-fur and red-laced dark blue sabretache.

54. RUSSIA: a) Ural cossack.
b) Cossack.
c) Officer, 4th Ukrainian Cossacks.

To this day the name 'cossack' (from the original Turkish 'quzzaq', adventurer) implies terror and savagery. Superb horsemen, these nomadic steppe-dwellers were an undisciplined, incredibly tough and wild body of irregular cavalry which gave unswervingly loyal service to the Czars. The impression they created was varied; their supporters described them as happy, faithful, good-natured and religious with a tendency to appropriate anything which took their fancy. Their detractors pictured them as the devil incarnate – brutal, merciless cutthroats who stole everything in sight but shrank from a man-to-man fight. The truth is probably somewhere in between. The French initially despised them, one officer claiming that a whole regiment of cossacks would not attack a skirmish-line of voltigeurs, an opinion which misunderstood the basic cossack tactic of operating in loose order, harrying the enemy's rear and flanks, riding-down stragglers and scouts, and cutting-up supply-trains. With such tactics there was no need to engage in costly conventional warfare. Even some Russian officers held them in low esteem, for example criticising Platov for avoiding action at Borodino, when in fact his elaborate manoeuvres paralysed the French left for over two hours with minimal Russian loss. As the campaign progressed blood-curdling stories of cossack barbarity were circulated so that in Germany prayers were offered: 'De Cossaquibus, Domine, libera nos!' ('Deliver us, Lord, from the cossacks'), and during the Retreat only the cossack cry of 'hurrah' was needed to throw entire divisions into panic.

The cossacks were organised into tribal groups or 'voiskos', with tribal chieftains or 'atamans' as officers and the 'hetman' (general) above all. A Prussian officer, Col. von Boyen, said that the cossack ought not to be judged 'by the standards of so-called civilised nations, because from this point of view [he] appears coarse and inclined to violence'; but seen as 'the child of nature', brought up 'exclusively to be a warrior', then other qualities are apparent. His endurance was mirrored in his rough little pony, 'mean in shape and slouching in motion' as General Wilson described, ill-conditioned and rugged but so hardy as to travel 'incalculable journeys, and remain exposed to the heat or cold, day or night, without manifesting any sense of inconvenience'. Von Boyen became quite carried away: 'the cossack is good-natured and loyal to his superiors . . . in unspoiled human nature there is a heart of gold, beside which our own culture appears to me a mere silver'. The opinion of a civilian whose entire property the cossacks had 'devoured or destroyed' (Wilson) or of a frozen, unarmed straggler facing a cossack lance would be somewhat different!

Contemporary descriptions of cossacks record similar details: fur cap with or without hanging bag 'in which he stuffs his provisions or other articles' (Wilson), loose blue jacket fastened by hooks 'with a white frog on the cuff or cape' (Wilson) or red 'around the cape and sleeves' (Sir R. Ker Porter), 'loose trousers with broad red stripe' (Porter), short boots, 'white or black Circassian short cloak' (Wilson), black cross-belts with 'tin cartouch box' (Porter), lance, brace of pistols, the universal whip, and sword either of the native 'kindjal' or 'shashqa' type or a conventional cavalry sabre, frequently captured from an enemy. 'An uncouth saddle is bound on the horse . . . like a doubled pillow, under which is a square piece of oil cloth painted in various colours' (Porter).

The 'Ural Cossack' in semi-'native' dress is taken from the Elberfeld Manuscript and has the typical large fur cap and 'mameluke' sword; the other trooper (from the same source) wears a long coat, red-striped trousers and the common peaked cap (see also Plate 4, *World Uniforms and Battles 1815–50*), sometimes worn without a peak. Sometimes seconded from the regulars, cossack officers often wore smarter uniforms; the 4th Ukrainian Cossack illustrated is taken from a René North drawing, based on contemporary material. The uniform includes a combination of fur cap and shako; the 1st, 2nd and 3rd Ukrainian wore similar costume but with crimson, scarlet and light blue facings respectively; the other ranks had more usual cossack costume.

55. a) BRITAIN: Trooper, 20th Light Dragoons.
b) RUSSIA: Cossack (Tartar).
c) RUSSIA: Crimean Tartar.

British participation in the 1812 campaign is generally unknown, the British contingent being restricted to the staff of General Wilson, official British observer, plus a corporal and four men of the 20th Light Dragoons (Wilson's old regiment). Wilson himself wore the conspicuous red staff uniform, often without an overcoat, though his dragoons were not so impervious to the cold; in December Wilson noted that 'my dragoons are chilled to the bone' and that he had been compelled to provide them with sheepskin coats. The trooper illustrated wears regimental uniform under the coat, of pre-1812 pattern (Wilson picked up his escort in Sicily en route to Russia, obviously before the British 1812 uniform had been issued), consisting of dark blue dolman with orange facings and yellow lace, grey service overalls, and fur-crested 'Tarleton' helmet with facing-coloured turban, with plume removed.

The tartars were a nomadic group originating from the Crimea, in appearance and organisation like the cossacks. The figure in the brown coat comes from the Elberfeld Manuscript, where it is titled 'Cossack aus den Tartarei'; the uniform worn under the fur-collared coat is green with red facings. The trousers are probably unbleached, and the sash a personalised addition. The second tartar is from a watercolour by Ludwig Wolf, showing the popular tall cloth cap, red-faced green coat with red cloth cartridge-tubes on the breast, and apparently a wooden saddle with folded blanket as described for Plate 54. Almost all contemporary pictures of cossacks show full beards; Dr Clarke, who travelled in Russia in the early nineteenth century, claimed that all Russians, from aristocracy to serfs, kept their hair 'universally in a state not to be described . . . only divested of vermin when they frequent the bath'. Countess Sophie Schwerin noted that the cossacks' first task on camping for the night was to clean their weapons, and then plaster their hair with the same oil!

General Wilson had a bodyguard

of cossacks and tells a story which illustrates the loyalty and naïevety of the ordinary cossack. Wilson's red uniform once attracted a French battery who began to fire roundshot at him. His cossack orderly rushed up and tried to replace Wilson's hat with his own fur cap; when reprimanded by his ataman for such disrespect, the cossack simply replied that the Englishman's hat and plume were attracting enemy fire, and as his duty was to protect General Wilson, he was only endeavouring to make himself the target!

56. RUSSIA: a) Kalmuk.
b) Bashkir.
c) Bashkir.

The Russian irregular cavalry included Asiatic tribes of Bashkirs and Kalmuks, even wilder than the cossacks and tartars, whose method of warfare was better fitted to the Dark Ages. Armed with bows and arrows and often wearing mail-coats and ancient helmets, the tribesmen were regarded with contempt by the French; Marbot stated that he knew of only one man killed by a bashkir arrow, though the enormous clouds of missiles they fired caused some serious wounds, a somewhat biased view. Marbot was himself wounded by a four-foot arrow fired from 'this ridiculous weapon'. The bashkirs, whose only tactic was a wild charge, 'helter-skelter like a flock of sheep' culminating in a volley of arrows, caused Marbot to wonder why the Russian government bothered to employ them, claiming that 'they only served to exhaust the country

and to starve the regular formations'; the French nicknamed them 'les Amours', a reference to the Cupid-like bows!

The bashkir dress included tall, fur-trimmed cap and long coat; Marbot states that many had no other weapons than the bow, but those illustrated (from the Elberfeld Manuscript) have a selection of firearms and sabres. One (perhaps a sub-chief) wears his bashkir hat and carries an ancient Turkish helmet (as shown by Horace Vernet). The Kalmuk (from the same source) wears a 'rabbit-ear' cap and one-piece trouser-boots. He carries the characteristic bow-case, often much larger than illustrated (a Schadow drawing shows a huge bow-case worn on the left of a bashkir's waist-belt, with the four-foot arrows mentioned by Marbot but shown shorter by other sources). Other bashkirs are shown with fur-trimmed hats of 'robin hood' style, one with a long brown coat bearing embroidered yellow flowers, blue sash and trousers and yellow-shafted lance (an almost Chinese dress), and another in all-yellow costume with crimson piping and zigzag trouser-stripe. Horse-furniture (and horses) were like those of the cossacks, with even cruder saddles and harnessing. Tribal chieftains sometimes had a medieval appearance with armour and ornate robes.

57. RUSSIA: a) Musketeer,
Infantry, winter.
b) Grenadier,
Infantry,
summer.

c) Musketeer, Infantry, 1812 regulation dress, summer.

Behaving and being treated like machines, the Russian infantry's ignorant but resilient spirit enabled it to take terrific punishment, to march for days and nights, to endure all manner of privations, and yet still behave with the 'obstinate bravery' described by General Wilson. Devotedly loyal to officers, country and Czar, they were 'religious without being weakened by superstition; patient, docile and obedient; possessing all the characteristics of a barbarian people, with the advantages engrafted by civilisation'. Initiative, however, was non-existent and the officers brave but indolent. John Spencer Stanhope thought the infantrymen 'made of a different stuff from other men . . . indeed, men of iron', but the officers 'negligent and inattentive to their duty'. Prior to the 1812 campaign a French officer spoke to him of the Russians: 'Ils sont des bêtes, mais on peut tuer une bête; Stanhope added, 'They are bêtes, however, that would take some killing'.

The regulations of 1 January 1812 introduced the distinctive 'kiwer' shako, but it seems certain that many units fought the campaign in their old uniforms. The double-breasted dark green jacket had the collar lowered and closed from 1812; its colouring is interesting. Later in the century it was usual to dye the soldiers' uniforms black, as black dye was more serviceable and the official dark green was almost that colour anyway; hence Tolstoy's references to 'black' uniforms. Evidence is inconclusive but it seems that in 1812 the genuine dark green shade was used.

Organisation varied from infantry to grenadier battalions, though basically the regiment consisted of three battalions, each of three musketeer and one grenadier company, the latter often detached to form composite grenadier units (in addition to the ordinary grenadier battalions). In practice the 3rd battalions were so weak as to be mainly used as depôt units; each battalion had an official establishment of 738 of all ranks. Grenadiers had three-flamed grenade badges on the shako and cartridge-box (musketeers had single-flamed grenades) and (from 1810) red shoulder-straps. The 1808 pattern 'stovepipe' shako originally had an enormous plume for grenadiers but thinner ones were used from February 1811; cords were added in June 1809, usually worn on campaign, often hooked up out of the way over the pompom. Pompoms were apparently in battalion colours: sources conflict but one states these were white with green centre for 1st Btns, green with white centre for 2nd and blue with white for 3rd. These decorations continued on the 'kiwer'.

From 1807 all infantry had red collars, cuffs and turnbacks, with shoulder-straps indicating the division to which the unit belonged and its seniority in the division. Legwear varied, some sources showing French-style white breeches and gaiters, though the official issue was of white, one-piece 'gaiter-trousers', with looser white overalls for winter, with button-on knee-length black leather gaiters, apparently slightly lengthened in 1812, carried on top of the knapsack when not in use. Equipment consisted of square leather knapsack, cartridge-box, iron mess-tin and sabre and bayonet in a combined frog; the greatcoat was rolled over one shoulder worn under the knapsack-strap from 1809. Haversacks and sometimes axes in cases were carried on campaign. Musket-slings were red-brown, and muskets often of lamentable quality: Dr Clarke stated that though the Imperial factory at Tula produced 1,300 muskets a week, 'the name of musquet is degraded by such things as they produce; it is wonderful any troops can use them: besides being clumsy and heavy, they miss fire five times out of six, and are liable to burst whenever they are discharged' (they were not as bad as Clarke claimed, but no less than 28 different calibres were in use, plus 60,000 fine English weapons given as rewards to selected soldiers)!

Shoulder-straps were red for the 1st Regiment of a division, 2nd white, 3rd yellow, 4th dark green piped red and 5th light blue; divisional numbers were embroidered in red (yellow on red straps). The following table lists Russian infantry regiments, the colour of shoulder-strap and the divisional number carried upon it:

Alexopol 12Y, Apsheron 9W, Archangel 8R, Azov 6R, Bieloserk 10G, Bielov 19Y, Bialystock 17W, Boutirki 24W, Brest 17Y, Briansk 6G, Chernigov 3R, Crimea 10Y, Dnieper 18Y, Estonia 14G, Galich 13Y, Kexholm 11R, Kabardinsk 20Y, Kaluga 5G, Kamenchatka 16Y, Kazan 19R, Kolyvan 15Y, Koporsk 3G, Koslov 15W, Kostroma 18G, Kourin 15G, Krenenchug 4Y, Kursk 10W, Lagoda 26W, Libau 7Y, Lithuania 21Y, Mingrelia 16G, Minsk 4G, Mohilev 5Y, Moscow 7W, Murmansk 3W, Nacheburg 9R, Narva 12W, Navajinsk 14Y, Neuschlot 16R, Neva 21R, Nishki-Novgorod 26R, Nisov 6Y, New-Ingermanland 12G, Odessa 11B, Okhotsk 16W, Old-Ingermanland 8Y, Olonetz 22G, Orel 27G, Penza 13G, Perm 5R, Pernov 11G, Petrovsk 21W, Podolsk 11Y, Polotsk 21G, Poltava 26Y, Pskov 7R, Revel 3Y, Riazan 17R, Riazsk 9Y, Riga 23R, Sebastopol 19G, Seleguinsk 23Y, Saratov 13W, Schlüsselburg 8W, Shirvan 24R, Sievsk 5W, Sofia 7G, Smolensk 12R, Suzdal 19W, Staroskol 22Y, Tambov 18W, Tenguinsk 14W, Tiflis 20W, Tobolsk 4R, Tomsk 24G, Troitsk 20R, Tula 14R, Ufa 24Y, Ukraine 8G, Uglich 6W, Veliki-Lutsk 13R, Vilmanstrand 17G, Vitebsk 15R, Vyburg 22R, Vilno 27W, Viazma 22W, Volhynia 4W, Vologda 19B, Vladimir 18R.

The white sword-knots had coloured parts to distinguish companies: 1st Company all-white, 2nd blue ball and head, 3rd orange ball and head, 4th green waist, 5th green ball, waist and head, 6th orange ball and head, green waist, 7th blue waist, 8th blue ball, waist and head, 9th orange ball and head, blue waist.

58. RUSSIA: a) Grenadier, 1812 uniform, summer.
b) Private, Moscow Grenadier Btn, campaign dress, with flag.

The Moscow Grenadier wears the

haversack used on campaign, and the long grenadier plume tied to the brown leather sword-scabbard by the shako-cords. He has the characteristic grey-brown greatcoat and waterproof shako-cover; the use of the latter was restricted but is shown by some contemporary pictures; for example a Georg Opitz watercolour of Russians entering Paris includes a man wearing a 'kiwer' with buff-coloured cover and N.C.O. pompom worn outside. The toggles attaching the knapsack to its straps can be seen in this plate.

The complex subject of Russian flags cannot be covered at length here; for details see the authoritative Zweguintzow title mentioned in the bibliography (a more accessible source is an article by Lt. Cmdr R. O. Morris in issue 36 of *Tradition*). Three basic patterns of infantry flag existed, restricted (from 1803) to two flags per battalion, all four arshins square (4 feet 8 inches):

1797 pattern. Orange central disc bearing black Imperial eagle with orb, sceptre and a shield on the breast bearing the St. George-and-Dragon motif, with a crown above and a wreath around, in gold and green embroidery respectively, all on the disc. Plain field with four 'rays' of contrasting colour from centre to each corner.

1800 pattern. More 'natural' eagle minus the breast-shield, surrounded by gold or silver wreath with large crown above; the 'rays' narrower and bearing the Imperial cypher in gold

or silver in the outer corners with gold crown above; above the eagle a light blue scroll bearing Cyrillic lettering 'God be with us' on one side and 'Thanks be to God' on the other. *1803 pattern.* As 1800 but 'rays' widened again, scrolls removed, and with the new cypher AI (Alexander I).

The pattern carried depended only upon the date of issue; poles were black for the 1803 pattern, previously brown, yellow, black or white, brass pike-heads bearing the Imperial eagle, and streamers of silver lace with interwoven black and orange thread.

Each battalion carried one 'white' and one 'coloured' flag. The 'white' 1797 flags had white field with coloured 'rays', but after 1800 were all-white except for the orange centre and embroidery. The 'coloured' flags had field and (sometimes two-coloured) 'rays' in contrasting shades. A fourth pattern was introduced in 1806, the 'Flags of St. George', awarded for outstanding service; like the 1803 style but the eagle's breast bearing the St. George emblem on a green circle (not all sources show this detail), with an inscription recording the award around the edges, and the streamer in the colours of the Order of St. George (orange with three black stripes).

The following table briefly describes the flags carried by the grenadier regiments at Borodino, of which the Moscow Btn illustrated was one:

Regt	Model	Field	'Rays' of 'Coloured' Flag	'Rays' of 'White' Flag
Arakcheev	1797	black	light green	black/light green
Pavlov	1797	orange	white	orange
Ekaterinoslav	1797	dark apricot	white/blue	dark apricot/blue
St. Petersburg	1797	poppy-red/white	poppy-red/white	poppy-red/white
Tavrichesk	1800	black	red	black/red
Kiev	1806	rose	white	white
Moscow	1803	black	red	white
Astrakhan	1797	apricot	white	apricot
Fanagoria	1803	rose	green	white
Siberian	1797	green/rose	black	black/green
Little Russian	1797	black	rose	black/rose

See also black-and-white plates.

59. RUSSIA: a) Musketeer company officer, 1812 uniform, summer.
b) Company officer, Grenadier Regt Pavlovski, full dress, 1813.
c) Grenadier, campaign dress.

Infantry officers wore similar uniform to their men, of better quality, with longer coat-tails, lace-edged epaulettes with flattish-ended 'crescents', bearing the divisional number in metal on the cloth strap, white 'gaiter-trousers', breeches and boots, or grey overalls with buttons down the outer seam, gorget, silver lace sash with interwoven black and orange 'flecks' (the sword-knot was similarly coloured), and 'kiwer' with silver cords and bullion tassels and silver lace pompom bearing a gold-embroidered Imperial cypher on an orange centre. Field officers

only had epaulette-fringes; in 1812 the shako-cords and sashes were ordered to be worsted instead of lace. Officers on campaign carried the knapsack.

The Guard regiments were the élite of the army; at Borodino Major-General von Löwenstern recorded the young soldiers of the Preobraschenski and Semenovski Guards preserving 'a truly military bearing . . . the shots were already working to devastating effect in their midst, but the men stood just as stoically and silently as before, with their muskets by their sides, and they coolly closed up their ranks whenever a missile claimed its victims . . .'. In the same action the colonel of the Ismailovski recorded 'the enemy fire destroyed our ranks . . . the lines simply closed up again and maintained their discipline . . .', whilst the Litovsk at one point actually bayonet-charged the French cavalry!

The Pavlovski officer wears the

1813 uniform, when the unit had been taken into the Guard; it is illustrated to show both the 'Guard' features (coloured lapels and the 'Garde-litzen' lace loops on collar and cuff-flaps) and the archaic regimental brass-fronted mitre caps stamped with the Imperial arms, with red cloth rear piped white and a white head-band bearing brass grenades. The pompom was either white or white with orange centre (sources conflict). The caps were handed down in the regiment so that in 1914 there were caps in use which had holes made by musket-balls in 1807! Lace was white for other ranks (see Plate 4, *World Uniforms and Battles 1815–50*). Other Guard units wore the 'kiwer' with copper double-eagle plate (gilt for officers); the cartridge-box bore a copper plate shaped as the Order of St. Andrew. The lace was yellow for the other regiments, whose collars were: Preobraschenski and Litovsk red, Semenovski and Guard Grenadiers light blue piped red, Ismailovski dark green piped red. A popular fashion was to leave the lower cuff-button unfastened.

The voluminous greatcoat was characteristic of the Russian infantry; the serf preferred loose clothing and the infantry frequently campaigned with the greatcoat worn over the shirt, the jacket being put into store. The British Captain Mercer noted in 1815 a popular style of wearing the greatcoat-skirts drawn back by means of a waist-belt, to free the legs of the restrictive skirts, a comfortable but untidy fashion. The cloth forage cap shown was introduced in September 1811, green with a band of the collar-colour and piping in 'company' colour; officers' caps had black leather peaks.

60. RUSSIA: a) Private, 36th Jägers.
b) Jäger.
c) N.C.O., 4th Jägers.

There were thirty-two Russian Jäger regiments until 1810, when numbers 33 to 46 were formed from fourteen line units; the number increased to fifty by 1812. The jäger uniform was like that of the infantry, but with green collars, cuffs and turnbacks with red piping, and black leather equipment. White 'gaiter-trousers' were worn in summer, and dark green breeches with red piping in winter. Officers' grey service overalls had a double black stripe. Shako-badges like the line; cartridge-boxes bore brass regimental numbers. Shoulder-straps were sky-blue for regiments except those numbered 1 to 11, 13, 15 to 20, 23, 27 to 31, and 49, which had yellow; these bore divisional numbers as the line.

All Russian N.C.O.s had rank-distinctions of metallic lace on the collar and cuffs, and 'quartered' black-and-white shako-pompom. The cane was a further distinction. The jäger in 'stovepipe' shako is taken from the Elberfeld Manuscript, dated January 1814 and apparently showing the pre-1812 cap still in use, though with 'new' jacket, with unusual flap-less cuffs. The cartridge-box has an unusual plate, apparently a circular brass disc bearing the Imperial eagle.

61. RUSSIA: a) Private, 3rd Marines, winter dress.
   b) Officer, Foot Artillery.
   c) Officer, Horse Artillery.

The Russian artillery drew enthusiastic comments from observers like General Wilson ('Their artillery is so well horsed, so nimbly and so handily worked, that it bowls over almost all irregularities of surface with an ease, lightness and velocity that gives it great superiority'). The dynamic young Major-General Kutaisov planned far-seeing tactics for handling guns in action, basically their concealment from the enemy until necessary and then using massed batteries to achieve a particular tactical objective. He tried to change the policy of withdrawing batteries when danger threatened: 'The artillery must be prepared to sacrifice itself. Let the anger of your guns roar out! Fire your last charge of canister at point-blank range! A battery which is captured after this will have inflicted casualties on the enemy which will more than compensate for the loss of the guns.' His gunners at Borodino obeyed these instructions, but Kutaisov forgot his duties and in his enthusiasm led a bayonet-charge near the Raevsky Redoubt, and was never seen again. His death meant that much of his concealed reserve was never ordered into action – a tragedy for the Russian army.

The Horse Artillery officer illustrated wears dragoon helmet and cavalry-pattern coatee, in the artillery colours of dark green with black facings and red piping, and service overalls; white breeches, riding boots and white gauntlets were worn in full dress. Dragoon-pattern shabraques were dark green with gold lace decoration. The Elberfeld Manuscript shows a gunner wearing leather reinforced overalls and a long, dark grey riding-cloak with red standing collar, one end thrown over the shoulder. The Foot Artillery officer wears pre-1812 pattern uniform, the shako-badges of crossed cannon-barrels over bursting grenade. The 1812 pattern uniform is shown in Plate 62.

Marines wore infantry uniform and equipment, with dark green facings and white piping. Shoulder-straps were coloured in the same system as the infantry: 1st Marines, red straps bearing yellow 25; 2nd, white bearing red 25; 3rd, yellow bearing red 25; 4th, green bearing red 28.

62. RUSSIA: a) Field Officer, Foot Artillery, full dress.
   b) Drummer, Foot Artillery, summer uniform.
   c) N.C.O., Foot Artillery, winter uniform.

The 1812-pattern Foot Artillery uniform was like that of the infantry, with black facings and red piping. Rank-distinctions like those of the infantry; the officer wears fringed epaulettes indicative of 'field' rank. Gunners wore red shako-cords. Artillery drivers wore the Foot Artillery shako and jacket, and leather-reinforced grey cavalry overalls.

The drummer illustrated (after Knötel) wears the style common to all Russian musicians, the ordinary uniform with lace loops on the breast, sleeves, rear seams and wings. The drummer's apron (as shown by Knötel) is much larger than usual, almost like that of a pioneer. Knötel also illustrates a bulkier sword-knot than normal. Regimental distinctions among Russian musicians naturally also existed. Drum-hoops were coloured in the national white-and-green triangles.

63. RUSSIA: a) Jäger, Russo-German Legion.
b) Hussar, Russo-German Legion.
c) Gunner, Horse Artillery, Russo-German Legion.

The Russo-German Legion was raised at Revel in August 1812 from captured German prisoners-of-war, principally Prussian. It initially consisted of one infantry battalion, one hussar regiment, one horse battery and one jäger company. Reinforced by more P.O.W.s, deserters and volunteers, its strength at the end of 1813 comprised seven infantry battalions, two hussar regiments, one foot and two horse batteries, one artillery train company and one jäger company. In March 1815 it transferred to Prussian service.

The only contemporary illustrations are in the Elberfeld Manuscript, dated March 1814 and perhaps showing items adopted after 1812.

The hussar wears a typical Russian costume, including 'kiwer', white-furred dark green pelisse with yellow braid, yellow sash with red barrels and red trouser-stripe (the 2nd Regt, when raised, wore an all-black dress with sky-blue facings, brown pelisse-fur and bell-topped shako with white cords and drooping plume). The gunner, wearing a foot artillery shako with brass crossed-cannons badge and cavalry overalls, possibly belonged to the train or could have been a driver for a foot battery. The jäger wears infantry uniform with interesting additions: the shako-plume, aiguillette, cartridge-box worn at the front and cross-belt badge.

The infantry wore Russian infantry uniform, with green or grey trousers, the 1st Brigade with red collars and the 2nd blue, battalions apparently differentiated by the shoulder-straps, the Elberfeld pictures showing red, and yellow with red piping. See Plate 74, *Uniforms of Waterloo*.

64. RUSSIA: a) 'Peasant cossack'.
b) Militiaman.
c) Partisan (peasant militia).

There were three auxiliaries to the Russian army. The 'opolchenie' – the official 'levée en masse' or militia – was usually organised into recognizable formations, the quality varying from reasonably equipped and armed to wretched companies wearing peasant clothing. Secondly were the partisan bands, consisting usually of cossacks and hussars, often small in number and used to harry the flanks and rear of the enemy, and to act as a nucleus for larger bodies formed locally from the 'opolchenie' and the third category, consisting of haphazard groups of peasants, armed with axes and clubs, who were responsible for most of the atrocities which befell the (mostly unarmed) stragglers from the 'Grande Armée'. Some used the excuse of protecting the motherland to justify the pillage and murder of harmless camp-followers.

Though often crudely-armed, the 'opolchenie' on occasion fought with the regulars: the Moscow and Smolensk 'opolchenie' were present at Borodino. General Wilson wrote of them at Maloyaroslavets: 'The very militia who had just joined (and who, being armed only with pikes, formed a third rank to the battalions) not only stood as steady under the cannonade as their veteran comrades, but charged the sallying enemy with as ardent ferocity', proof of the genuine patriotic fervour aroused by foreign invasion.

The uniform of the 'opolchenie' varied considerably; all were supposed to wear a loose garment like the peasant 'kaftan', with cloth or fur cap bearing a Maltese cross badge (later copied by the Prussian 'landwehr' militia). The variation illustrated is taken from the Elberfeld Manuscript and dated January 1814, showing the fur hat with brass badge and a great-coat or smock with red collar and shoulder-strap piping, and infantry equipment including cartridge-box bearing the Imperial eagle. A similar dress worn by a Russian militia unit at Leipsig in 1813 is described by the Swedish lieutenant Wossidlo: '. . . a shabby-looking unit; they wore rough grey coats without a collar and dirty cloth-caps . . .'. The Grande Armée's 27th Bulletin (October 1812) described '. . . on the field of battle 1700 Russians, amongst whom were 1100 recruits, dressed in grey jackets . . .'.

The Saxon Col. von Meerheimb, wounded at Borodino, was escorted as a prisoner by a kindly Russian officer, who 'whenever he met any armed peasants, who formed a reserve militia to transport, escort and guard prisoners, he always made a detour and gave me to understand that it was dangerous to fall into their hands . . . the appearance of these Russian militiamen was dreadful, and if they had worn long cowls of hide instead of dark brown and grey clothing, one would justifiably not have been able to tell them apart from deer. Many had so much hair on their faces that nothing was visible except the nose and eyes . . .'.

The cavalryman illustrated is described as 'Peasant Cossack' in the Elberfeld Manuscript, but possibly represents a partisan. The third figure is entitled 'Russian Coachman' in the Manuscript, obviously a civilian or irregular, wearing virtually a 'national costume'. Dr Clarke recorded the ordinary peasant costume: '. . . universally habited, in winter, in a jacket of sheep's hide, with the wool inwards; a square-crowned red cap, with a circular edge of black wool round the rim. These, with a long black beard, sandals made of the bark of the birch tree, and legs bandaged in woollen, complete the dress'.

It is interesting to note that the

bands of armed peasantry were viewed with some official suspicion, caused by fears that unsupervised partisans might turn to insurrection – in fact one partisan leader, Capt. Naryshkin, was ordered to disarm his own men and 'execute those convicted of rebellion'! This near-sighted policy reduced the number of partisans able to harry the French; one Private Chetvertakov, who singlehandedly raised a peasant force of between 300 and 4,000 in the Gzhatsk region from a patriotic desire to expel the French, was regarded as a troublemaker and was forced to return to his regiment.

PRUSSIA

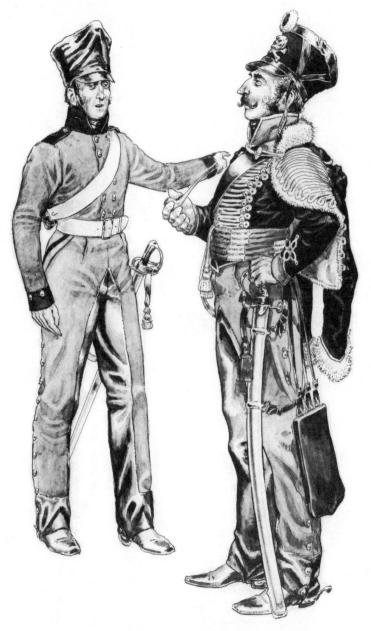

A a) Trooper Dragoons.
     b) Trooper, Leib-Hussars.

B a) Prussian Officer, 3rd Uhlans.
b) Austrian Dragoon Trooper.

C a)   Officer, Chevalier-Gardes, service dress.
      b)   Officer, Chevalier-Gardes, undress.

D a) Partisan officer.
   b) Artillery officer, service dress.

E   a) Guard Flag, 1800 pattern.
      b) Infantry Flag, 1803 pattern.

F a) Flag, 1st Infantry.
b) Flag, 2nd Btn, 13th Infantry.

G a) French Flag, 4th Btn, 7th Light Infantry.
   b) Italian Flag, 2nd Infantry.

H a) Flag, 1st Grenadiers, Imperial Guard.
   b) Flag, 7th Light Infantry.

I a) N.C.O., Artillery.
    b) Officer, Artillery.

J a) Trumpeter, 16th Lancers.
b) Pioneer, 7th Infantry.

THE BLACK AND WHITE PLATES

A. PRUSSIA: a) Trooper, Dragoons.
b) Trooper, Leib-Hussars.

The Prussian hussar shako was usually covered by a black 'water-proof'; pelisse-fur was white for troopers, black for N.C.O.s and grey for officers. Lace and shako-cords were of the button-colour, equipment

Dragoons' in 1812 were: 2nd (1st West Prussian) white, 3rd (Lithuanian) and 4th (2nd West Prussian) scarlet, and 5th (Brandenburg) black; buttons white for the 2nd and 4th and yellow for the others.

See also Plates 66, 67 and 68, *Uniforms of Waterloo*; and Plate 29, *Uniforms of the Napoleonic Wars*.

Regt	Dolman and Pelisse	Collar and cuffs	Buttons
1st (1st Leib-Hussars)	black	scarlet	white
2nd (2nd Leib-Hussars)	black	scarlet	white
3rd (Brandenburg)	dark blue	scarlet	white
4th (1st Silesian)	brown	yellow	yellow
5th (Pommeranian)	dark blue	dark blue	yellow
6th (2nd Silesian)	green	scarlet	yellow

black leather, and sashes of the facing colour with barrels of the button-colour. Officers had laced shoulder-straps on the pelisse and black-and-silver sashes. The white metal skull and crossed bones badge was exclusive to the Leib-Hussars. Colours of the 'Combined Hussar' corps were as listed above.

The 1st and 2nd Leib-Hussars had white and scarlet shoulder-straps respectively on the dolman.

The Prussian dragoon light blue 'kollet' had collar, cuffs, shoulder-straps and turnback-piping of the facing colour; covered shako and grey service overalls, the brass buttons on the seams of the latter having been abolished in 1811 but probably still worn in some cases. Facing-colours of the regiments forming the 'Combined

B. a) PRUSSIA: Officer, 3rd Uhlans.
b) AUSTRIA: Trooper, Dragoons.

Prussian Uhlans wore blue 'kollet' with scarlet collar, pointed cuffs, piping and turnback-edging, with shako bearing black-and-white national pompom and rosette and yellow cords. Officers wore the usual sash and other ranks a blue-and-red girdle; yellow metal buttons. The two regiments supplying squadrons to the 'Grande Armée' were distinguished by their shoulder-straps, the 2nd (Silesian) Regt having scarlet and the 3rd (Brandenburg) yellow. Lance-pennons red-over-blue for the 2nd and yellow-over-blue for the 3rd; officers of the latter also carried lances with white-lacquered shafts, and blue-over-yellow pennon larger than the troopers' version and bearing embroidered golden sun over a black Prussian eagle with gold crown and sword, over gold inscription NEC SOLI CEDIT. See also Plates 72/73, *Uniforms of Waterloo*.

Austrian dragoons wore their traditional white uniform with facing-coloured collar, cuffs and turnback-edging, and leather helmet with brass fittings and black-and-yellow crest. Grey overalls with leather buttons worn on campaign; white leather equipment with brass fittings.

C. RUSSIA: a) Officer, Chevalier-Gardes, service dress.
b) Officer, Chevalier-Gardes, undress.

The Chevalier-Gardes undress uniform consisted of dark green 'surtout' and breeches with silver epaulettes and buttons, minus lace and facings. The hat bore silver loop and tassels, orange-black-and-white cockade, and white-over-yellow plume. Officers also had a double-breasted red coatee with black facings, silver epaulettes and two silver 'Garde-litzen' loops on collar and cuffs, worn on public holidays and special social occasions. The functional dark green coat with black facings – similar to the Prussian 'litewka' – was worn on active service.

Knötel shows the infantry undress consisting of ordinary coatee with dark green breeches and knee-boots, bicorn with green feather plume, and no sash. Many Russian officers were notoriously lax about their appearance; on one occasion Kutuzov shouted angrily at a shabby raga-muffin riding nearby, 'What kind of scum are you?' The man yelled back: 'Captain of general staff Brosin, quartermaster of I Cavalry Corps!'

D. RUSSIA: a) Partisan officer.
b) Artillery officer, service dress.

The partisan officer is based on a portrait of the legendary Denis Davidov, an audacious regular officer who had witnessed the destruction of his family's estates at Borodino, and who commanded a band of forty hussars and eighty cossacks serving as the nucleus of his guerrilla force, composed mainly of armed peasants. The uniform is an imitation of tartar or cossack 'tribal' dress, with regulation sash and guard-less cossack sword. The mediaeval iron mace with flanged head is taken from a portrait of Hetman Platov by Orlowski.

The artillery officer is taken from a Schadow sketch, showing a campaign uniform including greatcoat-like garment with epaulettes, apparently an overcoat with lapels folded back rather than the frock-coat. The roughly-tied sash, mis-shapen cap and starched shirt-collar shown in the original perhaps indicate a deliberate 'Bohemian' appearance instead of the rigours of campaign.

E. RUSSIA: a) Guard Flag, 1800 pattern.
b) Infantry Flag, 1803 pattern.

See text to Plate 58. The 'Guard' flag

illustrated is that issued in 1800 to the Preobraschenski, Semenovski and Izmailovski Regiments (other Guard units had none until 1813). Design and colouring as described before, with metallic embroidery in gold; 'white' flags had poppy-red 'rays' and the 'coloured' flags were red with white 'rays' and narrow white upright cross; all three regiments used the same colouring but the Semenovski's colour-poles were black, Izmailovski's white, coffee-brown for the Preobraschenski's 'white' flag and straw-yellow for their 'coloured' flag. The Fanagorisky Grenadiers' 'Flag of St. George' bore gold-lettered details of the award around the edges.

F. POLAND: a) Flag, 1st Infantry.
b) Flag, 2nd Btn, 13th Infantry.

Flag of the 1st Infantry, captured by the Arsamass Dragoons at Borisov in 1812; crimson with white eagle, gold crown, orb, sceptre and lettering; silver standard-head with gilt crown and lettering. A written description recorded a white flag of this unit, bearing the French Republican cock and lettering REPUBLIQUE FRANCAISE on one side and LEGION POLONAISE on the other, an old flag like that shown in Plate 25. The flag of the 13th Infantry was white throughout, with gold embroidery, silver fringe, and painted panel representing a woman in a blue robe with Romulus, Remus and wolf at her feet, in natural colours. Standard-head as before but minus crown; gold cords. See text for Plate 24.

G. a) FRANCE: Flag, 4th Btn, 7th Light Infantry.
b) ITALY: Flag, 2nd Infantry.

Italian flag consisted of large white diamond bearing dark blue central disc, gold lettering and green branches underneath; corner segments red (upper left and bottom right) and dark blue. French flag is a regimental pattern, often attributed to the 4th Btn, 7th Polish Infantry, and captured at Viasma.

H. FRANCE: a) Flag, 1st Grenadiers, Imperial Guard.
b) Flag, 7th Light Infantry.

The 1st Grenadiers flag of 1811 issue, similar to 1804 pattern: white central diamond with alternate red and blue triangles, gold embroidery. The reverse probably repeated the lettering of 1804: VALEUR/ET DISCIPLINE/1er BATAILLON. The 7th Light Infantry flag (see Plate 49) of 1812 pattern: 'tricolor' design with gold embroidery and fringe. Lettering on reverse: L'EMPEREUR/NAPOLÉON/AU 7me RÉGIMENT/D'INFANTERIE/LÉGÈRE. 'Cravats' (streamers) of tricolor design with gold embroidery and fringe; gold cords also attached to pole.

I. WÜRTTEMBURG:
a) N.C.O., Artillery.
b) Officer, Artillery.

The Württemburg artillery wore black-crested leather helmet with brass plate and chinscales, light blue jacket with black collar, cuffs, and turnbacks (the latter with yellow grenade badge) and yellow piping, with N.C.O. lace on collar and cuffs, gold epaulettes for officers and black shoulder-straps piped yellow for other ranks. Legwear either light blue breeches and black gaiters, or on campaign grey overalls with black leather reinforcing with or without light blue stripes, officers having light blue overalls with double gold stripe. Faber du Faur's sketches of his unit on campaign show loose trousers with leather false boots, flat forage-caps, jackets like the infantry (see Plate 33) or with the exaggerated, turned-back lapels illustrated, and later in the campaign tattered, greatcoated figures with feet smothered in rags. See also Plate 75, *Uniforms of the Napoleonic Wars*.

J. POLAND: a) Trumpeter, 16th Lancers.
b) Pioneer, 7th Infantry.

The pioneer of the 7th has black bearskin with red plume, French cockade and brass plate (design presumed); white jacket with red collar and lapels, dark blue cuffs, flaps and turnbacks, all piped white; epaulettes with yellow strap, blue crescent and red fringe; white apron, belts, gauntlets and overalls; black gaiters; brass sword-hilt. Each unit wore different dress: the 4th's pioneers, for example, had the same cap but with number on the plate, red jacket with light blue collar, cuffs and turnbacks all piped white, yellow lapels and cuff-flaps piped light blue, yellow epaulettes with white fringe and blue crossed-axes badge on the upper arm.

The trumpeter has white peaked fur cap with red plume, brass chin-scales and plate with white metal eagle; all-white kurtka with crimson collar and turnbacks, white epaulettes and piping; medium blue overalls with crimson piping; white belt with brass plate, brass sabre-hilt, steel scabbard and white knot; brass trumpet with mixed crimson-and-white cords. The shako is Polish hussar pattern, of light blue cloth with leather fittings and silver decorations.

APPENDIX I

Order of Battle, Grande Armée

The following list was originally compiled from existing 'livrets de situations' (returns of strengths) dated between 25 May and 15 July 1812 ('Les effectifs de la Grande-armée pour la campagne de Russe de 1812', Paris 1913, and 'Adjutant's Call' of the Military Historical Society (U.S.A.) Vol. III). At best it is a provisional list as organisation and personalities changed throughout the campaign. All units are French unless stated otherwise.

HEADQUARTERS
(CHIEF OF STAFF: MARSHAL BÉRTHIER)
About 400 officers served in various Staff appointments.
Attached to H.Q.: Bataillon de Neuchâtel, 1 Btn (Swiss).
Guides of the General Headquarters, 1 Coy.
Gendarmerie Impériale, 1 Sqdn.

IMPERIAL GUARD (MARSHALS BESSIÈRES AND MORTIER)
1st Division (Delaborde)
Brig. Berthezène: 4th Tirailleurs, 4th and 5th Voltigeurs, 2 Btns each.
Brig. Lanusse: 5th and 6th Tirailleurs, 6th Voltigeurs, 2 Btns each.
2nd Division (Roguet)
Brig. Lanabèze: 1st Voltigeurs and 1st Tirailleurs, 2 Btns each.
Brig. Boyeldieu: Fusilier-Chasseurs, Fusilier-Grenadiers, Flanquers; 2 Btns each.
3rd Division (Lefevre)
Brig. Boyer: 1st and 2nd Chasseurs, 2 Btns each.
Brig. Curial: 1st, 2nd and 3rd (Dutch) Grenadiers, 2 Btns each.
Cavalry of the Guard
Grenadiers à Cheval, Chasseurs à Cheval, Dragoons, 5 Sqdns each.
Élite Gendarmes, 2 Sqdns; Mamelukes, 1 Coy.
1st (Polish) and 2nd (Dutch) Lancers, 4 Sqdns each.
Attached to the Guard
Portuguese Chasseurs à Cheval, 3 Sqdns; 7th Chevau-Légers-Lanciers, 4 Sqdns.
Velites du Prince Borghese (Italian), Velites of the Tuscan Guard (Italian), Spanish Engineers, 1 Btn each.

'*Division Claparede*'

    Brig. Chlopicki: 1st and 2nd Regts, Vistula Legion (Polish), 3 Btns each.

    Brig. Bronikowski: 3rd and 4th Regts, Vistula Legion (Polish), 3 Btns each.

    Note: The 4th Regt and the 3rd Btns of the others only joined during the Retreat. Bronikowski remained behind as Governor of Minsk.

FIRST ARMY CORPS (MARSHAL DAVOÛT)

1st Division (Morand)

    Brig. d'Alton: 13th Light Infantry, 5 Btns.

    Brig. Gratien: 17th Light Infantry, 5 Btns.

    Brig. Bonami: 30th Line, 5 Btns.

2nd Division (Friant)

    Brig. Dufour: 15th Light Infantry, 5 Btns.

    Brig. Vandedem: 33rd Line, 5 Btns.

    Brig. Grandeau: 48th Line, 5 Btns; Régt de Joseph-Napoléon (Spanish), 2 Btns.

3rd Division (Gudin)

    Brig. Gérard: 7th Light Infantry, 5 Btns.

    Brig. Desailly: 12th Line, 5 Btns.

    Brig. Leclerc: 21st Line, 5 Btns; 127th Line, 2 Btns; 8th Confederation Regt (Mecklenburg-Strelitz), 1 Btn.

4th Division (Dessaix)

    Brig. Barbanegre: 33rd Light Infantry, 4 Btns.

    Brig. Fréderichs: 85th Line, 5 Btns.

    Brig. Leguay: 108th Line, 5 Btns.

5th Division (Compans)

    Brig. Duppelin: 25th Line, 5 Btns.

    Brig. Teste: 57th Line, 5 Btns.

    Brig. Guyardet: 61st Line, 5 Btns.

    Brig.   : 111th Line, 5 Btns.

Corps Cavalry (Girardin)

    Brig. Pajol: 2nd Chasseurs à Cheval, 9th Lancers (Polish), 4 Sqdns each.

    Brig. Bourdesoulle: 1st and 3rd Chasseurs à Cheval, 4 Sqdns each.

SECOND ARMY CORPS (MARSHAL OUDINOT)

6th Division (Legrand)
Brig. Albert: 26th Light Infantry, 4 Btns.
Brig. Moreau: 56th Line, 4 Btns.
Brig. Maison: 19th Line, 4 Btns.
Brig. Pamplona: 128th Line, 3rd Portuguese Regt, 2 Btns each.

8th Division (Verdier)
Brig. Raymond-Vivies: 11th Light Infantry, 4 Btns; 2nd Line, 5 Btns.
Brig. Pouget: 37th Line, 4 Btns; 124th Line, 3 Btns.

9th Division (Merle)
Brig. Amey: 4th Swiss Regt, 3 Btns; 3rd Provisional Croatian Regt, 2 Btns.
Brig. Condras: 1st Swiss Regt, 2 Btns; 2nd Swiss Regt, 3 Btns.
Brig. Coustard: 3rd Swiss Regt, 3 Btns; 123rd Line, 4 Btns.

Corps Cavalry
Brig. Castex: 23rd and 24th Chasseurs à Cheval, 4 Sqdns each.
Brig. Corbineau: 7th and 20th Chasseurs à Cheval, 8th Chevau-Légers-Lanciers, 4 Sqdns each.

THIRD ARMY CORPS (MARSHAL NEY)

10th Division (Ledru)
Brig. Gengoult: 24th Light Infantry, 4 Btns; 1st Portuguese Regt, 2 Btns.
Brig. Marion: 46th Line, 4 Btns.
Brig. Bruny: 72nd Line, 4 Btns; 129th Line, 2 Btns.

11th Division (Razout)
Brig. Joubert: 4th and 18th Line, 4 Btns each.
Brig. Compère: 2nd Portuguese Regt, 2 Btns; Illyrian Regt, 4 Btns.
Brig. d'Henin: 93rd Line, 4 Btns.

25th Division (Marchand)
Brig. v. Hügel: 1st and 4th Württemburg Regts, 2 Btns each.
Brig. v. Koch: 2nd and 6th Württemburg Regts, 2 Btns each.
Brig. v. Brüsselle: 1st and 2nd Württemburg Jägers, 1st and 2nd Württemburg Light Infantry, 2 Btns each; 7th Württemburg Regt, 2 Btns.
Note: 7th Regt in Danzig until September, joining Bde in November.

Corps Cavalry (*Wollwarth*)

Brig. Mouriez: 11th Hussars, 4 Sqdns; 6th Chevau-Légers-Lanciers, 3 Sqdns.

Brig. v. Walsleben: 4th Württemburg Mounted Jägers, 4 Sqdns (Transferred to Brig. Mouriez, 23 June).

Leib-Chevaulegers (Württemburg), 4 Sqdns (Transferred to Brig. Beurmann).

Brig. Beurmann: 4th and 28th Chasseurs à Cheval, 4 Sqdns each.

Brig. v. Breuning: 1st Württemburg Chevaulegers, 4 Sqdns (Transferred to Brig. Beurmann).

3rd Württemburg Mounted Jägers, 4 Sqdns (Transferred to Brig. Subervie, II Cavalry Corps, April).

FOURTH ARMY CORPS (EUGÈNE)

Italian Guard (*Lecchi*): Royal Velites, Élite Regt, Conscripts of the Guard, 2 Btns each.

Guards of Honour, 1 Coy; Dragoon Guards, 2 Sqdns; Queen's Dragoons, 4 Sqdns.

13th Division (*Delzons*)

Brig. Huard: 8th Light Infantry, 2 Btns; 84th Line, 4 Btns.

Brig. Roussel: 1st Provisional Croatian Regt, 2 Btns; 92nd Line, 4 Btns.

Brig. Ferrier: 106th Line, 4 Btns.

14th Division (*Broussier*)

Brig. B. de Sivray: 18th Light Infantry, 2 Btns; 9th Line, 4 Btns.

Brig. Alméras: 35th Line, 4 Btns; Régt de Joseph-Napoléon (Spanish), 2 Btns.

Brig. Pastol: 53rd Line, 4 Btns.

15th Division (*Pino*)

Brig. Fontana: 1st Light Infantry (Italian), 1 Btn; 2nd Italian Line, 4 Btns.

Brig. Guillaume: 3rd Light Infantry (Italian), 4 Btns; Dalmatian Regt, 3 Btns.

Brig. Dembowski: 3rd Italian Line, 4 Btns.

Corps Cavalry

Brig. Guyon: 9th and 19th Chasseurs à Cheval, 3 Sqdns each.

Brig. Villata: 1st and 2nd Italian Chasseurs à Cheval, 4 Sqdns each.

FIFTH ARMY CORPS (PRINCE PONIATOWSKI)

16th Division (Zajonczek)

Brig. Mielzynski: 3rd and 15th Polish Regts, 3 Btns each.

Brig. Paszkowski: 13th and 16th Polish Regts, 3 Btns each.

Note: 13th left to garrison Zamosca; when Russians approached Duchy of Warsaw the unit formed nucleus of improvised division of militia and cavalry depot troops.

17th Division (Dombrowski)

Brig. Zoktowski: 1st and 6th Polish Regts, 3 Btns each.

Brig. Pakosz: 14th and 17th Polish Regts, 3 Btns each.

18th Division (Kamieniecki; from July, Kniaziewicz)

Brig. Grabowski: 2nd and 8th Polish Regts, 3 Btns each.

Brig. Wierbinski: 12th Polish Regt, 3 Btns.

(later, St. Potocki)

Corps Cavalry (Kaminski; from September, Sébastiani, later Lefebvre-Desnöettes)

Brig. Tyszkiewicz: 4th Polish Chasseurs à Cheval, 4 Sqdns.

Brig. Kaminski: 1st Polish Chasseurs à Cheval and 12th Polish Lancers, 4 Sqdns each.

Brig. Sulkowski: 5th Polish Chasseurs à Cheval and 13th Polish Hussars, 4 Sqdns each.

SIXTH ARMY CORPS (MARSHAL GOUVION ST. CYR)

19th (Bavarian) Division (Deroy)

Brig. Siebern: 1st and 9th Regts, 2 Btns each; 1st Light Infantry, 1 Btn.

Brig. Raglowicz: 4th and 10th Regts, 2 Btns each; 2nd Light Infantry, 1 Btn.

Brig. Rechberg: 8th Regt, 2 Btns; 6th Light Infantry, 1 Btn.

20th (Bavarian) Division (Wrede)

Brig. Vincenti: 2nd and 6th Regts, 2 Btns each; 2nd Light Infantry, 1 Btn.

Brig. Beckers: 3rd and 7th Regts, 2 Btns each; 4th Light Infantry, 1 Btn.

Brig. Habermann: 5th and 11th Regts, 2 Btns each; 5th Light Infantry, 1 Btn.

(from 25 May, Scherer)

Corps Cavalry (detached 15 July to form a division under Preysing)

Brig. Seydewitz: 3rd and 6th Bavarian Chevaulegers, 4 Sqdns each.

Brig. Preysing: 4th and 5th Bavarian Chevaulegers, 4 Sqdns each.

SEVENTH ARMY CORPS (GENERAL REYNIER)

21st (Saxon) Division (Lecoq)

Brig. Steindel: Regts Prinz Friedrich and Prinz Clemens, 2 Btns each; Liebenau Grenadier Btn.

Brig. Nostiz: Regt Prinz Anton, 3 Btns; 1st Light Infantry, 2 Btns.

22nd (Saxon) Division (Gutschmidt; from June, Funck)

Brig. v. Sahr: Grenadier Btns v. Anger and v. Spiegel, 1 Btn each; 2nd Light Infantry, 2 Btns.

Brig. v. Klengel: Regts König and Niesemeuschel, 2 Btns each; Grenadier Btn Eychelberg (left at Praga, Warsaw).

Corps Cavalry

Brig. Gablentz: Regts Polenz and Prinz Clement (Saxon), 4 Sqdns each; Saxon Hussars, 8 Sqdns.

EIGHTH ARMY CORPS (JÉRÔME; ultimately JUNOT)

23rd (Westphalian) Division (Tharreau)

Brig. Damas: 2nd Regt, 3 Btns; 6th Regt, 2 Btns; 3rd Light Infantry, 1 Btn.

Brig. Wickenberg: 3rd and 7th Regts, 3 Btns each; 2nd Light Infantry, 1 Btn.

24th (Westphalian) Division (Ochs)

Brig. Legras: Chasseur-Carabiniers, Guard Chasseurs and Guard Grenadiers, 1 Btn each; 1st Light Infantry, 1 Btn; 5th Regt, 2 Btns.

Corps Cavalry

1st and 2nd Westphalian Hussars, Westphalian Guard Chevaulegers, 4 Sqdns each.

Westphalian Garde du Corps, 1 Coy. (Returned to Germany with Jérôme).

NINTH ARMY CORPS (MARSHAL VICTOR)

12th Division (Partouneaux)

Brig. Billiard: 10th and 29th Light Infantry, 1 Btn each.

Brig. Camus: 44th Line, 2 Btns; Provisional Line Regt formed from 1 Btn of each of the 36th, 51st and 55th Line.

Brig. Blammont: 125th Line, 3 Btns; 126th Line, 4 Btns.

26th Division (Daendels)

Brig. Damas: 1st, 2nd and 4th Berg Regts, 2 Btns each; 3rd Berg Regt, 1 Btn.

Brig. Hochberg: 1st, 2nd and 3rd Baden Regts, 2 Btns each; Baden Light Infantry Btn.

Brig. Prinz Emil: Leibgarde and Leib-Regt (Hesse-Darmstadt), 2 Btns each; 8th Westphalian Regt, 2 Btns; Hesse-Darmstadt Garde-Fusiliers, 2 Btns (this unit part of Danzig garrison, joined 26th Division during campaign).

28th Division (Girard)

Brig.   : 4th, 7th and 9th Polish Regts, 3 Btns each.

Note: 3rd Btns of these units joined on 28 September.

Brig. Klengel: Regts v. Low and v. Rechten (**Sax**ony), 2 Btns each.

Corps Cavalry (Fournier)

Brig. Delâtre: Berg Lancers and Hesse-Darmstadt Chevaulegers, 3 Sqdns each.

Brig. Fournier: Regt Prinz Johann (Saxony) and Baden Hussars, 4 Sqdns each.

TENTH ARMY CORPS (MARSHAL MACDONALD)

7th Division (Grandjean)

Brig. Bachelu: 5th Polish Regt, 4 Btns.

Brig. Radziwill: 10th and 11th Polish Regts, 4 Btns each.

Brig. Ricard: 13th Bavarian Regt and 1st Westphalian Regt, 2 Btns each.

27th (Prussian) Division (Yorck)

Brig. Below: 1st Combined Regt (2nd Btn 1st Regt, 1st Btn 3rd Regt, Fusilier Btn 1st Regt).

    2nd Combined Regt (1st Btn 4th Regt, 1st and Fusilier Btn 5th Regt).

    Fusilier Btn 3rd Regt (not mobilised until June).

Brig. Horn: 3rd Combined Regt (2nd and Fusilier Btns 2nd Regt, 1st Btn 10th Regt).

        Leib-Regiment (9th).

Brig. Raumer: 5th Combined Regt (1st Btn 6th Regt, 1st and Fusilier Btns 7th Regt).

        6th Combined Regt (2nd Btn 11th Regt, 1st and Fusilier Btns 12th Regt).

Unattached: East Prussian Jäger Btn.

Corps Cavalry (Prussian)

Brig. Jeanneret: 3rd Combined Hussars (1st and 3rd Sqdns 4th Hussars, 1st and 2nd Sqdns 6th Hussars).

        1st Combined Hussars (3rd and 4th Sqdns 1st

Hussars, 2nd and 3rd Sqdns 2nd Hussars).

Brig. Huenerbein: 1st Combined Dragoons (1st and 2nd Sqdns 4th Dragoons, 2nd and 4th Sqdns 3rd Dragoons).

2nd Combined Dragoons (1st and 3rd Sqdns 2nd Dragoons, 1st and 3rd Sqdns 5th Dragoons).

ELEVENTH ARMY CORPS (MARSHAL AUGERAU)

30th Division (*Heudelet*)

Brig.　　　　　: 1st Provisional Regt, 3 Btns.

Brig.　　　　: 6th Provisional Regt, 4 Btns.

Brig.　　　　　: 7th Provisional Regt, 3 Btns; 8th, 9th and 17th Provisional Regts, 4 Btns each.

31st Division (*LaGrange*)

Brig.　　　　　: 10th Provisional Regt, 4 Btns; 11th Provisional Regt, 3 Btns.

Brig.　　　　　: 12th Provisional Regt, 4 Btns; 13th Provisional Regt, 3 Btns.

32nd Division (*Durutte*) (Joined VII Corps at end of Retreat)

Brig. Antheiny: Regts de Belle Isle and de Walcheren (French penal corps, 3 Btns each); 7th Confederation Regt (Würzburg), 3 Btns; Würzburg Chevaulegers, 1 Sqdn.

Brig. Maury:　Regt de Rhé (French penal corps, 3 Btns); 1st and 2nd Mediterranean Regts (Italian), 3 Btns each.

33rd Division (*Destrées*)

Brig. Rossaroll: Marines and Velites (Naples), 4 Btns.

Brig. Ambrosio: 5th, 6th and 7th Regts (Naples), 2 Btns each.

Brig.　　　　: Guards of Honour and Velites (Naples), 4 Sqdns.

34th Division (*Morand*, later *Loison*)

Brig.　　　　: 22nd Light Infantry, 2 Btns.

Brig. Lacroix: 3rd, 29th, 105th and 113th Line, total 10 Btns.

Brig.　　　　: 3rd Confederation Regt (Frankfurt), 3 Btns.

Brig. Anting: 4th Confederation Regt, 3 Btns; 5th Confederation Regt (Anhalt and Lippe), 2 Btns; 6th Confederation Regt (Schwarzburg, Waldeck and Reuss), 2 Btns.

Brig.　　　　: Regt Prinz Maximilian (Saxon), 3 Btns.

4th Westphalian Regt (marched with 34th Div. before transferring to VI Corps).

Corps Cavalry

4 Sqdns composed from one company from each of the French Dragoon Regts numbered 2nd, 5th, 12th, 13th, 14th, 17th, 19th and 20th.

FIRST CAVALRY CORPS (GENERAL NANSOUTY)

1st Light Cavalry Division (Bruyers)

Brig. Jacquinot: 7th Hussars and 9th Chevau-Légers-Lanciers, 4 Sqdns each.

Brig. Piré: 8th Hussars and 16th Chasseurs à Cheval, 4 Sqdns each.

Brig. Niemojewski: 6th and 8th Polish Lancers, 4 Sqdns each; 2nd Combined Hussars (Prussian) (1st and 3rd Sqdns 5th Hussars, 3rd and 4th Sqdns 4th Hussars).

1st Heavy Cavalry Division (St. Germain)

Brig. Bessières: 2nd Cuirassiers, 4 Sqdns.

Brig. Bruno: 3rd Cuirassiers, 4 Sqdns.

Brig. Queunot: 9th Cuirassiers, 4 Sqdns; 1st Chevau-Légers-Lanciers, 3 Sqdns.

5th Heavy Cavalry Division (Valence)

Brig. Reynaud: 6th Cuirassiers, 4 Sqdns.

Brig. Dejean: 11th Cuirassiers, 4 Sqdns.

Brig. de la Grange: 12th Cuirassiers, 4 Sqdns; 5th Chevau-Légers-Lanciers, 3 Sqdns.

SECOND CAVALRY CORPS (GENERAL MONTBRUN)

2nd Light Cavalry Division (Sébastiani)

Brig. St. Geniez: 11th and 12th Chasseurs à Cheval, 4 Sqdns each.

Brig. Burthe: 5th and 9th Hussars, 4 Sqdns each.

Brig. Subervie: 10th Polish Hussars, 3 Sqdns; Prussian Combined Lancers (3rd and 4th Sqdns 3rd Uhlans, 3rd and 4th Sqdns 2nd Uhlans).

2nd Heavy Cavalry Division (Wathiez de St. Alphonse)

Brig. Caulaincourt: 5th Cuirassiers, 4 Sqdns.
(later Beaumont)

Brig. Richter: 8th Cuirassiers, 4 Sqdns.

Brig. Dornez: 10th Cuirassiers, 4 Sqdns; 2nd Chevau-Légers-Lanciers, 3 Sqdns.

4th Heavy Cavalry Division (Defrance)

Brig. Berkheim (later Chouard): 1st Carabiniers, 4 Sqdns.

Brig. l'Héritier (later Paultre): 2nd Carabiniers, 4 Sqdns.

Brig. Ornano (later Bouvier): 1st Cuirassiers, 4 Sqdns; 4th Chevau-Légers-Lanciers, 3 Sqdns.

THIRD CAVALRY CORPS (GENERAL GROUCHY)
3rd Light Cavalry Division (Castel)

Brig. Gauthrin: 6th Hussars and 8th Chasseurs à Cheval, 4 Sqdns each.

Brig. Gérard: 6th and 25th Chasseurs à Cheval, 4 Sqdns each.

Brig. Dommanget: 1st and 2nd Bavarian Chevaulegers and Regt. Prinz Albert (Saxony), 4 Sqdns each.

3rd Heavy Cavalry Division (attached to II Corps) *(Doumerc)*

Brig. Berkheim: 4th Cuirassiers, 4 Sqdns.

Brig. l'Héritier: 7th Cuirassiers, 4 Sqdns.

Brig. Doullembourg: 14th Cuirassiers, 4 Sqdns; 3rd Chevau-Légers-Lanciers, 3 Sqdns.

6th Heavy Cavalry Division (Lahoussaye)

Brig. Thiry: 7th and 23rd Dragoons, 4 Sqdns each.

Brig. Serou: 28th and 30th Dragoons, 4 Sqdns each.

FOURTH CAVALRY CORPS
(GENERAL LATOUR-MAUBOURG)
4th (Polish) Light Cavalry Division (Rozniecki)

Brig. Dziewanowski: 2nd, 7th and 11th Lancers, 3 Sqdns each.

Brig. Turno: 3rd, 15th and 16th Lancers, 3 Sqdns each.

7th Heavy Cavalry Division (Lorge)

Brig. Thielemann: Saxon Garde du Corps and Saxon Zastrow Cuirassiers, 4 Sqdns each; 14th Polish Cuirassiers, 2 Sqdns.

Brig. Lepel: 1st and 2nd Westphalian Cuirassiers, 4 Sqdns each.

AUSTRIAN AUXILIARY CORPS
(PRINCE SCHWARTZENBERG)
Cavalry Division (Frimont)

Brig. Schmelzer: Hohenzollern and O'Reilly Dragoons, 8 Sqdns each; Erzherzog Dragoons, 6 Sqdns.

Brig. Frolich: Kaiser and Hessen-Homburg Hussars, 8 Sqdns each.

Brig. Zeichmeister: Blankenstein and Kienmayer Hussars, 8 Sqdns each.

Division Bianchi
Brig. Hesse-Homburg: Regts Hiller and Colloredo-Mansfeld, 2 Btns each; Grenadier Btn Kirchenbetter.
Brig. Lilienberg:　　　Regts Simbschen and Alvinzy, 2 Btns each; Grenadier Btn Brezinski.

Division Siegenthal
Brig. Bolza:　　　7th Jäger Btn; Warasdiner Border Infantry, 2 Btns.
Brig. Mohr:　　　Regts Prinz de Ligne and Czartoryski, 2 Btns each.
Brig. Lichtenstein: Regts Daidovitz and Sottulinski, 2 Btns each.

Division Trautenberg
Brig. Pflacher: 5th Jäger Btn; Sankt Georger Border Infantry, 2 Btns.
Brig. Mayer:　Regt von Würtzburg, 4 Btns.

APPENDIX II

Order of Battle, Russian Army at Borodino, 7 September 1812

Note: all infantry regiments consisted of two battalions.

HEADQUARTERS
ACTING CHIEF OF STAFF: BARON BENNIGSEN

FIRST WEST ARMY (GENERAL BARCLAY DE TOLLY)

FIRST CORPS (LT. GEN. BAGGOVUT)
4th Division (Prince Eugène of Württemburg)
 1st Brigade: Tobolsk and Volhynia Regts.
 2nd Brigade: Krenenchug and Minsk Regts.
 3rd Brigade: 4th and 34th Jägers.
17th Division (Lt. Gen. Alsufev)
 1st Brigade: Riazan and Belozersk Regts.
 2nd Brigade: Brest and Vilmanstrand Regts.
 3rd Brigade: 30th and 48th Jägers.

THIRD CORPS (LT. GEN. TUCHKOV)
1st Grenadier Division (Lt. Gen. Stroganov)
 1st Brigade: Lifeguard and Arakcheev Grenadiers.
 2nd Brigade: Pavlovski and Ekatineroslav Grenadiers.
 3rd Brigade: St. Petersburg and Tavrichesk Grenadiers.
3rd Division (Gen. Konovnitsyn)
 1st Brigade: Revel and Murmansk Regts.
 2nd Brigade: Chernigov Regt; Seleguinsk Regt from 23rd Division
 3rd Brigade: 20th and 21st Jägers.
 Attached forces
  11th Jägers (from 7th Division).
  41st Jägers (from 12th Division).
  Two combined Grenadier Btns.
  Cossacks (Maj. Gen. Karpov).
  Moscow opolchenie.

FOURTH CORPS (LT. GEN. OSTERMANN-TOLSTOI)
11th Division
 1st Brigade: Kexholm and Pernov Regts.

2nd Brigade: Polotsk and Elets Regts.
3rd Brigade: 1st and 33rd Jägers.
23rd Division
   1st Brigade: Rylsk and Ekaterinburg Regts.
   2nd Brigade: 18th Jägers.
   Attached forces
     Korporsk Regt.
     1st Combined Grenadier Btn (from Regts of 17th Division).
     2nd Combined Grenadier Btn (from Regts of 11th and 23rd Divisions).

FIFTH CORPS (GRAND DUKE CONSTANTINE)
1st Lifeguard Division (Lt. Gen. Lavrov)
   1st Brigade: Preobrazhenski and Semenovski Regts.
   2nd Brigade: Ismailovski and Litovsk Regts.
   3rd Brigade: Lifeguard Jägers and Finland Guard Jägers.
   Attached: 2nd Combined Grenadier Division.
1st Cuirassier Division
   Chevalier Gardes.
   1st Brigade: Emperor's and Empress's Regts of Guard Cuirassiers.
   Attached: Lifeguard Dragoons (from 1st Cavalry Division).

SIXTH CORPS (GEN. DOKHTUROV)
7th Division (Lt. Gen. Kapsevich)
   1st Brigade: Pskov and Moscow Regts.
   2nd Brigade: Libau and Sofia Regts.
   3rd Brigade: 36th Jägers.
24th Division (Maj. Gen. Likhachev)
   1st Brigade: Shirvan and Boutirki Regts.
   2nd Brigade: Ufa and Tomsk Regts.
   3rd Brigade: 19th and 40th Jägers.

FIRST CAVALRY CORPS (LT. GEN. UVAROV)
1st Cavalry Division
   1st Brigade: Guard Lancer Regt. (Lifeguard Dragoons detached to Fifth Corps).
   2nd Brigade: Lifeguard Hussars and Lifeguard Cossacks.
   4th Brigade: Njeschin Dragoons.
   Attached: Elisavetgrad Hussars (from 2nd Cavalry Division).
Cossacks (Platov)

Ilovaisk, Grekov, Khartonov, Denisov and Zhirov Regts;
Simferol Tartars.

SECOND CAVALRY CORPS (MAJ. GEN. KORFF)
6th Brigade: Moscow and Pskov Dragoons.
8th Brigade: Iziumsk Hussars and Polish Lancers.
9th Brigade: Kurland and Orenburg Dragoons.
10th Brigade: Siberien and Irkutsk Dragoons.
11th Brigade: Sumski and Mariupol Hussars.

THIRD CAVALRY CORPS (MAJ. GEN. KREUTZ)
1st Brigade: Alexandrinsk Hussars and Siberian Lancers.
2nd Brigade: Smolensk Dragoons.

SECOND WEST ARMY (GEN. PRINCE BAGRATION)

SEVENTH CORPS (LT. GEN. RAEVSKY)
12th Division (Maj. Gen. Vasil'chikov)
1st Brigade: Smolensk and Narva Regts.
2nd Brigade: Alexopol and New-Ingermanland Regts.
3rd Brigade: 6th Jägers.
26th Division (Maj. Gen. Paskievich)
1st Brigade: Lagoda and Poltava Regts.
2nd Brigade: Nishki-Novgorod and Orel Regts.
3rd Brigade: 5th and 42nd Jägers.

EIGHTH CORPS (LT. GEN. BOROZDIN)
2nd Grenadier Division
1st Brigade: Kiev and Moscow Grenadiers.
2nd Brigade: Astrakhan and Fanagoria Grenadiers.
3rd Brigade: Siberian and Little Russian Grenadiers.
27th Division (Lt. Gen. Neverovsky)
1st Brigade: Odessa and Tarnopol Regts.
2nd Brigade: Vilno and Simbirsk Regts.
3rd Brigade: 49th and 50th Jägers.
Attached: 7th Combined Grenadier Division (Maj. Gen.
Vorontsov).

FOURTH CAVALRY CORPS (MAJ. GEN. SIEVERS)
4th Cavalry Division
12th Brigade: Kharkov and Chernigov Dragoons (both dismounted).

13th Brigade: Kiev and New Russian Dragoons.

14th Brigade: Akhtyrka Hussars and Litovski Lancers.

2nd Cuirassier Division

2nd Cuirassier Brigade: Ekaterinoslav and Military Order Regts.

3rd Cuirassier Brigade: Ghlukov, Little Russian and Novgorod Regts.

APPENDIX III

SOME UNIFORMS NOT ILLUSTRATED

The 'Confederation' Regiments

The smaller states of the Confederation of the Rhine supplied contingents so small that several had to be combined to form composite units. Uniforms and equipment by 1812 were of French pattern, though possibly some which took French uniform in that year may have worn older patterns.

3rd Regiment (Frankfurt-am-Main).
Dark blue uniform with red facings and piping; white shako-cords and buttons; dark blue legwear; cockade red-and-white.

4th Regiment (Saxon Duchies); cockade green-and-white for all.

Total strength 2,800; contingents from:

Saxe-Weimar and Saxe-Hildburghausen: green uniform with yellow collar-patch, white (summer) or grey (winter) trousers; white shako-cords; black leather equipment.

Saxe-Coburg: green jacket with yellow collar and cuffs, red turnbacks, three white lace loops on green cuff-flap; tight light blue breeches with yellow braid; short black gaiters; white shako-cords.

Saxe-Gotha-Altenburg and Saxe-Meiningen: dark blue faced red; white shako-cords and breeches; black gaiters.

5th Regiment (Anhalt-Lippe).

Anhalt-Dessau (350 men), Anhalt-Bernburg (240) and Anhalt-Köthen: green single-breasted jacket faced and piped rose-pink; white buttons; grey gaiters; red and green epaulettes, shako-cords and pompoms for grenadiers and voltigeurs respectively; black leather equipment; green cockade.

Schaumburg-Lippe (150) and Lippe-Detmold (500): white uniform with green collar, cuffs, turnbacks, piping; white breeches, buttons and shako-cords; cockade red-and-yellow for Schaumburg-Lippe and red-and-white for Lippe-Detmold.

6th Regiment.

Schwarzburg-Rudolstadt and Schwarzburg-Sonderhausen, two companies (350 men each): dark green jacket, red collar, cuffs, turnbacks and piping; grey breeches (grey with red stripe or green for officers); red plume; black leather equipment; cockade white-and-blue.

Waldeck, three companies (400 men): white uniform, dark blue collar, cuffs and lapels; yellow buttons; grey breeches; white equipment and shako-cords (from 1812 yellow cords and double-pompom); cockade black-and-yellow.

Reuss, three companies (450 men): white Austrian-style uniform, light blue collar, cuffs and breeches, the latter with yellow stripe and 'Austrian knot' on thigh; yellow shako-cords; red plume; white equipment; cockade black-red-yellow.

7th Regiment (Würzburg).

White uniform, red collar, cuffs, turnbacks, and lapels; white breeches and equipment; grenadiers and voltigeurs with red and green-and-yellow epaulettes and plumes respectively.

8th Regiment (Mecklenburg).

Mecklenburg-Strelitz (400 men) and Mecklenburg-Schwerin (1,900): single-breasted dark blue jacket, red collar, cuffs and turnbacks; grey breeches; white equipment; red and green epaulettes, plume and shako-cords for grenadiers and voltigeurs respectively. Cockade blue-yellow-red.

See figs. 219, 223, 224 and 226, *Military Uniforms of the World in Colour*.

Würzburg Chevaulegers

Single-breasted green jacket with red facings and shako-cords, red-over-black plume.

Dalmatian Regt (Kingdom of Italy)

Organised as light infantry and raised in 1806, the Dalmatian Regt. wore an unusual uniform: single-breasted dark green short jacket, red pointed cuffs and collar (yellow collar for voltigeurs), white waistcoat, dark green tight ankle-length breeches and native sandals ('opanche') as footwear. Shako adopted 1806, plate with letters R.D. stamped out, red pompom for carabiniers, chasseurs green and voltigeurs yellow. Shako and equipment of French style.

SOURCES AND BIBLIOGRAPHY

The bibliography below does not pretend to be exhaustive. Titles listed are those either consulted in the compilation of this book, or those of interest for further research on the campaign. Where an eye-witness description has been directly taken from a more modern work, the original source of the quotation is also listed below. Wherever possible, details of English language editions are given. A good, basic picture of the campaign can be obtained from the Brett-James's *1812*, Chandler's *Campaigns of Napoleon*, Duffy's *Borodino* and Palmer's *Napoleon in Russia*.

The 1812 Campaign

Adam, A., *Aus dem Leben eines Schlatenmalers*, Stuttgart, 1886.

Bertin, G., *La Campagne de 1812 d'après des témoins oculaires*, Paris ,1895.

Bigot, C., *Gloires et Souvenirs Militaires*, Paris, 1894. (Extracts from earlier works.)

Bonaparte, N., *Confidential Correspondence of Napoleon Bonaparte with his Brother Joseph*, London, 1855.

Bourgoing, P. de, *Souvenirs Militaires du Baron de Bourgoing 1791–1815*, Paris, 1897.

Boyen, H. von, *Denkwürdigkeiten und Erinnerungen 1771–1813*, Stuttgart, 1899.

Brandt, H. von, *Souvenirs d'un Officier polonais*, Paris, 1877.

Brett-James, A., *1812*, Macmillan, London, 1966. (Eye-witness accounts.)

Brett-James, A., *Europe Against Napoleon*, Macmillan, London, 1970. (Eye-witness accounts of the Leipsig campaign.)

Butkevicius, *Napoléon en Lithuanie, La Revue de Paris*, 1932.

Cary, J., *Remarks on Napoleon Bonaparte's Expedition to Moscow*, London, 1813.

Chandler, D., *The Campaigns of Napoleon*, Weidenfeld & Nicholson, London, 1967.

Chlapowski, D., *Mémoires sur les Guerres de Napoléon, 1806–13*, Paris 1908.

Clarke, Dr E. D., *Travels in Various Countries of Europe*, Cambridge, 1810.

Combe, Col., *Mémoires du Colonel Combe*, Paris, 1896.

Compans, J.-D., *Le Général Compans*, Paris, 1912.

Costello, E., *Adventures of a Soldier; written by himself*, London, 1852; reprinted Longmans, London, 1967.

De Las Cases, Count, *Memoirs of the Life, Exile and Conversations of the Emperor Napoleon*, London, 1836. (Interesting but biased!)
Delderfield, R. F., *The Retreat from Moscow*, Hodder & Stoughton, London, 1967.
Douglas, R. B., *From Valmy to Waterloo*, Everett, London, 1906.
Duffy, C., *Borodino and the War of 1812*, Seeley Service, London, 1972.
Dumas, M., *Mémoires du Lieutenant-Général Matthieu Dumas de 1770 à 1836*, Paris, 1889.
Dupuy, R. E., and Dupuy, T. N., *Encyclopedia of Military History*, Macdonald, London, 1970.

Ellis, J., *A Short History of Guerilla Warfare*, Ian Allan, London, 1975.
Esposito, V. J., and Elting, R., *Military History and Atlas of the Napoleonic Wars*, Faber & Faber, London, 1964.

Fallou, L., *La Garde Impériale*, Paris, 1901.
Förster, F., *Geschichte der Befreiungskriege 1813, 1814, 1815*, Berlin, 1890.
Förster, F., *Preussen und Deutschland unter der Fremdherrschaft 1807–13*, Berlin.

Henckens, J. L., *Mémoires se rapportant à son service militaire au 6ème Régiment de Chasseurs à Cheval français de février 1803 à 1815*, La Haye, 1910.
Hogendorp, Gen. van, *Mémoires du Général Dirk van Hogendorp*, La Haye, 1887.

Kircheisen, F. M. (ed.), *Wider Napoleon! Ein deutsches Reiterleben 1806–15*, Stuttgart 1861/1911.

Labaume, E., *Circumstantial Narrative of the Campaign in Russia*, London, 1814.
Lachouque, H., and Brown, A. S. K., *The Anatomy of Glory*, Lund Humphries, London, 1962.
Lossberg, F. W. von, *Briefe in die Heimath geschrieben während des Feldzuges 1812 in Russland*, Cassel, 1844.

Marbot, Baron, *Memoirs*, Longmans, London, 1913.

Markham, F., *The Bonapartes*, Weidenfeld & Nicholson, London, 1975.

Masson, F., *Cavaliers de Napoléon*, Paris, 1895.

Meerheimb, F. L. A. von, *Erlebnisse eines Veteranen der grossen Armee während des Feldzuges in Russland, 1812*, Dresden, 1860.

Mercer, Gen. C., *Journal of the Waterloo Campaign*, Blackwood, London, 1870.

Olivier, D., *The Burning of Moscow*, Allen & Unwin, London, 1964.

Palmer, A., *Napoleon in Russia*, Deutsch, London, 1967.

Palmer, A., *Russia in War and Peace*, Weidenfeld & Nicholson, London, 1972.

Pils, F., *Journal de Marche du Grenadier Pils*, Paris, 1895.

Porter, Sir R. Ker., *Travelling Sketches in Russia and Sweden*, London 1808.

Quennevat, J. C., *Atlas de la Grande Armée*, Paris, 1966.

Roeder, H., *The Ordeal of Capt. Roeder*, Methuen, London, 1960.

Roos, N. U. L. von, *Ein Jahr aus meinem Leben . . . mit der grossen Armee Napoleons, im Jahre 1812*, St. Petersburg, 1832.

Schlosser, L. W. G., *Erlebnisse eines sachsischen Landpredigers in den Kriegsjahren von 1806 bis 1815*, Leipsig, 1846.

Schreckenstein, Gen. Baron R. von, *Die Kavallerie in der Schlacht an der Moskwa am 7 September 1812*, Münster, 1858.

Schwerin, S., *Ein Lebensbild aus ihren eigen hinterlassenen Papieren*, Leipsig, 1911.

Ségur, Comte P. de, *History of Napoleon's Expedition to Russia*, London, 1825.

Spencer Stanhope, J., *Memoirs of A. M. W. Pickering. Together with extracts from the Journals of her Father John Spencer Stanhope, describing his Travels and Imprisonment under Napoleon*, London, 1903.

Suckow, K. von, *Aus meinem Soldatenleben*, Stuttgart, 1862.

Thirion, A., *Souvenirs militaires, 1807–18*, Paris, 1892.

Villatée des Prugnes, R., 'Les effectifs de la Grande Armée pour la Campagne de Russe de 1812', *Revue des études Historiques*, Paris, 1913.

Wilson, Sir R., *Brief Remarks on the Character and Composition of the Russian Army, and a Sketch of the Campaigns in Poland in the Years 1806 and 1807*, London, 1810.

Wilson, Sir R., *Narrative of Events during the Invasion of Russia by Napoleon Bonaparte, and the Retreat of the French Army*, London, 1860.

Wilson, Sir R. (ed. Brett-James, A.), *General Wilson's Journal 1812–14*, London, 1964.

Anonymous, *The Court and Camp of Buonaparte*, London, 1829.

Lettres interceptées par les Russes durant la campagne de 1812, Paris, 1913.

Uniforms

Note: The student should be wary of the accuracy of modern illustrations which are unaccompanied by either a large passage of text or a note of original sources.

Bukhari, E., *French Napoleonic Infantry*, Almark, London, 1973.

Chelminski, J. von, and Malibran, A., *L'Armée du Duche de Varsovie, 1807–15*, Paris, 1913.

Devaux, P., *Les Aides-de-Camp sous le 1er Empire*, Le Briquet, Orléans.

Fieffé, *Histoire des Troupes Étrangerès au Service de la France*, 1854.

Gembarzewski, B., *Wojsko Polskie 1807–14*, Warsaw, 1905/1967.

Haythornthwaite, P. J.; Cassin-Scott, J., and Fabb, J., *Uniforms of the Napoleonic Wars*, Blandford Press, Poole, 1973.

Haythornthwaite, P. J., *Uniforms of Waterloo*, Blandford Press, Poole, 1975.

Haythornthwaite, P. J., *World Uniforms and Battles 1815–50*, Blandford Press, Poole, 1976.

Haythornthwaite, P. J., *Weapons and Equipment of the Napoleonic Wars*, Blandford Press, Poole, 1979.

Head, M. G., *Foot Regiments of the Imperial Guard*, Almark, London, 1972.

Head, M. G., *French Napoleonic Artillery*, Almark, London, 1970.

Head, M. G., *French Napoleonic Lancer Regiments*, Almark, London, 1971.

Kannik, P., *Military Uniforms in Colour*, Blandford Press, Poole, 1968.

Knötel, R.; Knötel, H., and Sieg, H., *Handbuch der Uniformkunde*, Hamburg, 1937/1964.
Krijitski, A., *L'Armée Russe de 1812 à 1815*.

Lachouque, H., *Dix Siècles de Costume Militaire*, Paris, 1963.
Leinhart, Dr, and Humbert, R., *Les Uniformes de L'Armée Française*, Paris.
Linder, K., *Wojsko Polskie*. Warsaw.

Martin, P., *Der Bunte Rock*, Stuttgart, 1963; English edition, *European Military Uniforms*, Spring Books, London, 1967.
Martinet, P., *Galerie des Enfants de Mars*, Paris, c.1812.
Mollo, B., *Uniforms of the Imperial Russian Army*, Blandford Press, Poole, 1979.
Mollo, J., *Military Fashion*, Barrie & Jenkins, London, 1972.
Murray, W. H., *The Imperial Russian Army 1805–15*, New York.

Pivka, O. von, *Napoleon's German Allies – Westfalia and Kleve-Burg*, Osprey, London, 1975.
Pivka, O. von., *Napoleon's Polish Troops*, Osprey, London, 1975.

Quennevat, J. C., *Les Vrais Soldats de Napoléon*, Paris, 1968. (Many eye-witness illustrations.)

Riehn, R. K., *The French Imperial Army*, New York, 1961.

Seaton, A., *The Austro-Hungarian Army of the Napoleonic Wars*, Osprey, London, 1973.

Teuber, O., and Ottenfeld, R., *Die Österreichische Armee*, Vienna, 1895–1904.
Thorburn, W. A., *French Army Regiments and Uniforms*, Arms & Armour Press, London, 1969.

Viscovatov, V., *Description of the Historical Uniforms and Arms of Russian Troops*, St. Petersburg, 1841–62.

Young, Brig. P., *Chasseurs of the Guard*, Osprey, London.

Zweguintzow, W., *Drapeaux et Étandards de l'Armée Russe, XVIe Siecle à 1914*, Paris, 1964.

Plates

La Grande Armée de 1812, plates by Carle Vernet, ed. R. & J. Brunon.
Uniformkunde, R. Knötel.
L'Armée Française, L. Rousselot.
Soldats et Uniforms du Premier Empire, plates by J. Girbal, published by Dr F. G. Hourtoulle, Paris.
Heer und Tradition series.
Le Plumet series ('Rigo' – A. Rigondaud).
Paint-Your-Own cards, René North.
Les Uniformes du 1er Empire, various artists, ed. Cmdt E. L. Bucquoy.
Le Manuscrit d'Elberfeld, J. M. Bueno, 1967.

Artists

Works by the following contemporary artists were consulted:
Albrecht Adam, Leopold Beyer, Nicholas-Toussaint Charlet, George Dawe, Christian G. Faber du Faur, Peter Hess, Johann Adam Klein, Lameau & Misbach, Baron Louis-François Lejeune, Pierre Martinet, Georg Opitz, Grenadier Pils, Alexander Sauerweid, Gottfried Schadow, Peter Schulten, Christoph & Cornelius Suhr, J. F. Swebach, Carle Vernet, C.-F. Weiland, Ludwig Ulrich Wolf, and others.

In addition to those whose works are listed under 'Plates' (above), the following more modern artists were also consulted:
'JOB' (J. Onfroy de Bréville), E. Leliepvre, A. L. V. Moltzheim, V. V. Vereschagin, and others.

Periodicals

The following periodicals, among others, were consulted:

Royal Military Chronicle, London, 1812–13.
Tradition, International Society of Military Collectors.
Journal, Society Napoleonic.
Adjutant's Call, Military Historical Society, U.S.A.
Le Briquet, Amicale des Collectionneurs de Figurines Historiques du Centre Loire.